ISLAMIC SURVEYS 4

A HISTORY OF ISLAMIC SPAIN

by

W. MONTGOMERY WATT

with additional sections on literature by

PIERRE CACHIA

EDINBURGH
at the University Press

Edinburgh University Press
22 George Square, Edinburgh

First published 1965
Reprinted 1967
Paperback edition 1977
Reprinted 1992

Printed and bound in Great Britain by Page Bros (Norwich) Ltd.

A CIP record for this book is available from the British Library

ISBN 0 7486 0847 8

FOREWORD

In 1939 the prospect of a war which would involve many Asian nations made men in positions of responsibility in Britain suddenly aware of the meagre number of our experts in Asian languages and cultures. The Scarbrough Commission was set up, and its report led to a great expansion of Oriental and African studies in Britain after the war. In the third decade after 1939 events are making clear to ever-widening circles of readers the need for something more than a superficial knowledge of non-European cultures. In particular the blossoming into independence of numerous African states, many of which are largely Muslim or have a Muslim head of state, emphasises the growing political importance of the Islamic world, and, as a result, the desirability of extending and deepening the understanding and appreciation of this great segment of mankind. Since history counts for much among Muslims, and what happened in 632 or 656 may still be a live issue, a journalistic familiarity with present conditions is not enough; there must also be some awareness of how the past has moulded the present.

This series of "Islamic surveys" is designed to give the educated reader something more than can be found in the usual popular books. Each work undertakes to survey a special part of the field, and to show the present stage of scholarship here. Where there is a clear picture this will be given; but where there are gaps, obscurities and differences of opinion, these will also be indicated. Full and annotated bibliographies will afford guidance to those who want to pursue their studies further. There will also be some account of the nature and extent of the source material.

While the series is addressed in the first place to the educated reader, with little or no previous knowledge of the subject, its character is such that it should be of value also to university students and others whose interest is of a more professional kind.

The transliteration of Arabic words is essentially that of the second edition of *The Encyclopaedia of Islam* (London, 1960, continuing) with three modifications. Two of these are normal with most British Arabists, namely, *q* for *ḳ*, and *j* for *dj*. The third is something of a novelty. It is the replacement of the ligature used to show when two consonants are to be sounded together by an apostrophe to show when they are to be sounded separately. This means that *dh*, *gh*, *kh*, *sh*, *th* (and in non-Arabic words *ch* and *zh*) are to be sounded together; where there is an apostrophe, as in *ad'ham*, they are to be sounded separately. The apostrophe in this usage represents no sound, but, since it only occurs between two consonants (of which the second is *h*), it cannot be confused with the apostrophe representing the glottal stop (*hamza*), which never occurs between two consonants.

W. Montgomery Watt
GENERAL EDITOR

CONTENTS

CONTENTS

Note that chapters 5, 2; 9, 1; and 10, 3 are by Dr Cachia.

LIST OF ILLUSTRATIONS

Plates

Maps

ACKNOWLEDGMENTS

Plates 1, 2, 3, 4, 6, 8, 9, 10, 11, 12, 13, 14, 15, 16 and 17 are reproduced from *Moorish Spain* by Enrique Sordo by kind permission of the publishers, Elek Books, Ltd. Photographer, Wim Swaan. Plates 5 and 7 are reproduced by kind permission of the Victoria and Albert Museum.

A HISTORY OF ISLAMIC SPAIN

Introduction

THE INTEREST OF ISLAMIC SPAIN

FOR many centuries Moorish Spain has stirred the imagination of Europe. Ballads gave glamour to the courageous stand of Roland in the pass of Roncesvalles, while legends surrounded the figure of the Cid and made him a great hero. Nor was it merely the struggle against the Moors which caught the imagination. The better-informed inhabitants of the rude Christian kingdoms and dukedoms of western Europe realised that south of the Pyrenees was a land of higher culture, where amid material luxury men enjoyed the delights of music and poetry; and they gradually took over what they could of this culture. With the romantic movement something of the old admiration was revived, and it is doubtless through the influence of Washington Irving that "Alhambra" has become a familiar word to many who know nothing of the fourteenth-century palace.

Even for the prosaic scientific historian, who speaks of Islamic Spain—strictly, "Muslim" applies only to persons—the subject is not without its fascination. Here an oriental culture has entered Europe and left behind magnificent architectural remains. It offers an important example of the close contact of diverse cultures, and one that has contributed to making the European and American historian what he is. The chief monuments of this culture are relatively easy to visit, and in most seasons the visit is delightful. Moreover the study of Islamic Spain gives answers to questions regarding the general nature of historical processes. Such questions will guide the treatment of the subject in the present work, and may be briefly indicated here under three heads.

Firstly, Islamic Spain must be looked at in itself. It is commonly regarded as having great and magnificent achievements to its credit. But in what did its greatness consist? The loveliness of the buildings it has left? Works of pure literature that are major contributions to the world's store? Philosophical, scientific, or religious writings with a secure place among the classics of the "one world" into which we are moving? Or is this image of Islamic Spain largely dependent on the contrast between its luxury and the bareness of contemporary life in the rest of western Europe, and on the fact that it was the channel through which elements of higher culture, both material and intellectual, entered Europe?

Secondly, Islamic Spain must be looked on as a part of the Islamic world. It shared in the culture of a vast area, and the character of its links with the heartlands must be looked at. How did it keep in touch? Was it mainly a passive recipient or did it make any distinctive contribution to Islamic culture as a whole? May it be regarded as an active cell in the body-social of Islam? On the other hand, how far had it become adapted to the special circumstances of the Iberian peninsula, such as climate, geography and the mingling of religions? Did it manage to integrate the various racial and social groups into a unity, and to impregnate the whole society with its values? A subordinate question is that of the relation of Spain to North Africa, especially the part which is now Morocco and Algeria. How far were the two regions a single cultural area dominated by Spain?

Finally, Islamic Spain was in close contact with its European neighbours. What exactly did it contribute to Europe? In how many spheres can we trace its influence, and see where Europeans have learned from Spanish Muslims? Again, Europe has clearly been influenced by reacting against Islamic Spain. The crusade is in part a retort to the *jihād* or holy war of the Moors; and the Reconquista was a major formative element in the making of modern Spain. The answer to these last questions belongs to the history of Europe and of Christian Spain, but some indication will be given of the lines along which the answers must go.

(I)

THE MUSLIM CONQUEST

1. *The Conquest as a Phase of Arab Expansion*

To the inhabitants of Spain the Arab conquest in the years from 711 to 716 came as a bolt from the blue. For the Arabs themselves, however, the overrunning of Spain was merely one phase in a long process of expansion.[1] It was an eminently profitable and successful phase, and the success came very rapidly; but in the process of expansion which had begun at least as early as 630 there had been comparable phases. During the reign of the caliph ʿUmar (634–44) the embryonic Arab state—at this time an alliance of many, but not yet all, of the tribes of the Arabian peninsula—had defeated the Byzantine empire and wrested from it the provinces of Syria and Egypt, and had dealt such a crushing blow to the Persian empire that it ceased to exist, leaving what we now call Iraq and Persia to be occupied by the Arabs as soon as they could find men to hold them securely. And this was only a beginning. For about a century the Arabs continued to move onwards and outwards. One line of expansion was north-east along the golden road to Samarqand and beyond, and another south-east into the Indus valley, while in the west they progressed through the coast-lands of North Africa. The advance was not gradual but rather by a series of jumps. There were periods of quiescence and consolidation, when the Arabs paused in the face of some serious obstacle or in order to deal with internal tensions.

To understand how this amazing expansion was possible it is necessary to go back to the career of Muḥammad. Muḥammad was both prophet and statesman—a combination which modern man with his compartmentalised religion finds difficult to understand. As a statesman he was interested in Arab unity; but he may also have felt that political unity was implicit in the fact that his mission as a prophet was to the Arabs in general and not simply to the men of Mecca. Unity, however, was virtually impossible without expansion, because of the nature of nomadic life. The main economic basis of this life was the breeding and pasturing of animals, with irregular movements from those areas where pasture was abundant after rain to those where there were permanent wells. When they were in a position to do so the nomads exacted payments for the safe conduct of men and merchandise. Life was never easy in the Arabian desert, however, and a normal feature of it was the raid or razzia, which was usually aimed at driving off an enemy's animals but occasionally involved loss of human life. Deaths in the razzias and other fighting must have done something to reduce pressure on the limited food supplies. At some point in Muḥammad's career it must have become clear to him that, if there was to be a political unity of the Arabs, fighting and razzias would have to be suppressed; but this would increase the pressure on the available food. How could this difficulty be surmounted?

It is in this context that the Islamic conception of the *jihād* or holy war must be considered. It was never a purely religious phenomenon but always at least in part a political instrument. It was indeed a transformation of the nomadic custom of the razzia, immediately relevant to the conditions when Muḥammad controlled only Medina and a few allied tribes. The ordinary tribe might carry out a razzia against any tribe or family with which it was not for the moment on friendly terms. The little state of Medina functioned in many ways as a tribe. Among the nomadic tribes of the region it had its allies and friends and likewise its enemies. At least in the latter part of his career Muḥammad insisted that those who wanted to be full allies must become Muslims and accept him as prophet. In this situation the conception of the holy war meant that the raiding propensities of Muḥammad's followers were directed against non-Muslims; but as more of the tribes near Medina became Muslims it also meant that raiding parties had to go farther afield. There are indications that Muḥammad was aware that the growth of his alliance, by stopping raiding between the members of the alliance, was increasing the pressure on food supplies, and that he made preparations for more extended razzias into Syria, the nearest comparatively rich country. Certainly his successors, as soon as they had regained control over some disaffected tribes, directed large raiding expeditions against both Syria and Iraq.

It is a common misapprehension that the holy war meant that the Muslims gave their opponents a choice "between Islam and the sword". This was sometimes the case, but only when the opponents were polytheists and idol-worshippers. For Jews, Christians and other "people of the book", that is, monotheists with written scriptures—and the phrase was very liberally interpreted—there was a third possibility; they might become a "protected group", paying a tax or tribute to the Muslims but enjoying internal autonomy. A member of such a group was known as a *dhimmī*. Within Arabia the nomadic tribes were nearly all idolaters, and were therefore forced to become Muslims. Outside Arabia, however, the local inhabitants were expected to become "protected groups". There was no pressure to become Muslims, but rather to remain as they were. Movable booty captured on expeditions could be divided among the participants in the expedition, but when the Arab Muslims began to conquer land, they had no desire to divide it up among themselves and to settle down to an agricultural life. It was more advantageous to allow the existing cultivators to continue to cultivate, while the tribute and rents, divided among the Muslims, enabled them to be a full-time expeditionary force.

It was in this way that the Arabs were able to expand so rapidly and to keep on expanding. The full citizens or Muslims received a stipend from the treasury and were able to devote themselves almost wholly to soldiering. Since their stipend could be increased by a share of any booty captured, they were eager to go on expeditions which promised to be lucrative and not too arduous or dangerous. Where the raided populations submitted and became "protected", however, it was necessary to plan expeditions that went further afield, and also to leave garrisons in the main cities of the territories that had submitted to the Muslims.

The Arab expansion westwards had begun almost as soon as they had obtained a lodgement in Syria. From Syria an expedition had gone south-west into Egypt and between 640 and 642 brought the country under Arab control. Almost immediately afterwards there had been exploratory expeditions along the coast into Cyrenaica and Tripolitania. An attempted Byzantine come-back and their own preoccupations elsewhere slowed the progress of the Arabs, but in 670 they were able to found the city of Cairouan in Tunisia. Here again the advance was halted, chiefly because of the resistance of the Berber tribes, though the city of Carthage also remained in Byzantine hands. By playing on the rivalries between the Berber tribes, especially that between the nomads and the sedentary tribes, the Arabs were eventually able to establish themselves securely in Tunisia, while most of the Berbers accepted Islam. In 698 the Byzantines were finally driven from Carthage, and soon after 700 expeditions of Arab and Muslim (probably nomadic) Berbers began to penetrate through Algeria into Morocco and the Atlantic sea-board. The resistance of the sedentary Berbers of these regions was crushed, and they were forced to acknowledge Arab suzerainty. The closing stages in this advance to the Atlantic were the work of Mūsā ibn-Nuṣayr, who is said to have been appointed independent governor of Ifrīqiyya (i.e. Tunisia) in 708, responsible directly to the caliph in Damascus; previously the head of the administration in Cairouan had been subject to the governor of Egypt.

After these successes in north-west Africa it is conceivable that the Arabs might have continued southwards. In some directions at least there was terrain of the kind to which they were accustomed. Undoubtedly, however, the desire for booty was an important motive with the rank and file of the Muslims; and it must soon have become clear that the rewards of pushing further south-west or south would be meagre. On the other hand, there must have been rumours and half-reliable reports of the great wealth and wonderful treasures of Spain; and it is therefore not surprising that the Muslims decided to risk the entirely novel and distinctly hazardous operation of crossing the strait in order to discover what substance there was in the reports. The expansion into Spain was thus entirely in keeping with the previous extension of Arab power in North Africa, and might well have come about even had there been no factors in the local situation (such as the attitude and interests of Count Julian) to encourage them and give them an opening.

While the chief control remained in the hands of men of Arab race (reckoned solely on the male side), after the submission of the Berbers of Tunisia and eastern Algeria about 700, much of the man-power in the expeditions was Berber. Without this accretion of man-power the conquest of Spain would have been impossible. It is thus more correct to speak of Muslim expansion than of Arab expansion. Yet the distinction between Arabs and Berbers did not disappear when the latter became Muslims, and was to prove a grave source of internal tension in Islamic Spain.

2. *The Weakness of Visigothic Spain*

The Spain which was conquered so easily by the Muslims suffered from grave internal weaknesses. Not merely for an understanding of the conquest, however, but also for a proper appreciation of the whole cultural development of Islamic Spain, it is necessary to look at the condition of the Iberian peninsula in the early years of the eighth century.[2]

The Visigoths first entered Spain in 414 and occupied the north-east of the country—the Roman province of Tarraconensis. Thereafter they maintained their hold under various political arrangements, but there was no real unity because the Visigoths adhered to the heretical Arian form of Christianity, while the majority of the indigenous population was Catholic. An important change took place, however, in 589, when the king and the leading Visigoths abandoned Arianism for Catholicism. This helped in the establishment of a stable and unified kingdom embracing the whole Iberian peninsula and the province of Septimania in the south of France. By the beginning of the eighth century the Visigothic aristocracy and the Hispano-Roman nobles seem to have been fused together in a single privileged group which may be referred to as the "upper classes" (*clasas elevadas*). There were party divisions within the upper classes, but they do not seem to have followed strictly racial lines. To the upper classes belonged the ecclesiastical hierarchy. The archbishops and bishops played a considerable part in the governing and administering of the kingdom, but it was not a theocratic state, though that has sometimes been asserted. On the contrary, the bishops were dominated by the king and his advisers, and had largely ceased to represent the interests of the ordinary people.

The monarchy itself, however, was far from strong. The king was supposed to be elected by the upper classes from among their own number. There was thus no fixed law of succession, though some kings tried to secure the succession of a son by associating him with them in power before their deaths. This was often resented by the other members of the upper classes. Indeed there were constant intrigues over the succession. The king's weakness was due also to the unsatisfactory nature of his army. In theory, all free men capable of bearing arms had an obligation to serve, when summoned by the king. This was not the type of obligation and vassalage found under the feudal system which arose in western Europe in later centuries, but one where each man stood in direct relation to the king and owed him loyalty. Towards the end of the seventh century the kings were apparently finding great difficulty in collecting an adequate army. These unsatisfactory features of the monarchy appear to go back to the Germanic conception of the "tribe" or political unit, which the Visigoths in Spain were trying to apply to circumstances for which it was not suited.

Besides the upper classes the population comprised the Hispano-Romans of free status and also a large proportion of serfs as peasants, successors of the Roman coloni. The latter had a very difficult life, but even the free men felt themselves to be underprivileged. There was therefore much discontent, and many of the ordinary people looked on the Muslims as liberators and gave them all the assistance they could. The cities in particular had fared much worse under the Visigoths than under the Romans, and had lost many of their municipal privileges. Perhaps it was difficult for the Visigoths, because of their primitive background, to appreciate the benefits of commerce and of city life generally; but the chief reason was probably the general economic regression after the fall of the Roman empire.

This lack of appreciation of the need for commerce may be one of the factors underlying the harsh treatment accorded to the Jewish groups in the kingdom, for many of the Jews were merchants. Another factor was the close association of the bishops and the king; much of the work of governing the kingdom was transacted in church councils, and the ecclesiastical authorities, influenced naturally by theological considerations, looked upon the Jews as enemies. Specially harsh decrees of the council of 693 made it virtually impossible for the Jews to continue as merchants. Many then entered into conspiracy with their Jewish associates in North Africa, and in 694 a further decree enslaved all who did not accept baptism. Even if this was subsequently relaxed and not strictly carried out, the strong feelings among the Jews may have encouraged the Muslims to invade, and the North African Jews were doubtless ready to give what information they possessed. Once the Muslims had defeated the Visigothic army, the Jews certainly gave them all the help they could.

The immediate prelude to the invasion was a customary quarrel about the succession, except that this quarrel had plunged the peninsula into what was practically civil war. A father and son had reigned since 687. The son, Witiza, wanted one of his sons, Akhila, to succeed, and to mark him out appointed him *dux* of the north-east province (Tarraconensis). When Witiza died in 710, a strong group of nobles seem to have elected Roderick king, but Akhila appears to have retained his province and even to have minted coins as if he were an independent sovereign. Thus Roderick was not in secure control of all the kingdom when he had to meet the Muslim invaders, and it is not surprising that he was defeated, and that after his defeat there was no individual or group capable of acting as central authority of the kingdom.

The weakness of the Visigothic kingdom may thus be attributed to three main factors: the divisions within the upper classes over the succession to the kingship; the discontent of the other sections of society at the privileges of the upper classes, with the consequent unreliability of the army; and the persecution of the Jews.

3. *The Course of the Invasion*, 711–716

It was in April or May 711 that the first substantial body of Muslims set foot in southern Spain, and saw Andalusia in its most attractive mood.[3] This was not quite the earliest Muslim contact with Spain, but what went before can be discerned only dimly through a haze of legend. *Faute de mieux* we must start from this legend. The central figure is a count Julian, about whose very name there have been fierce arguments. He was possibly a Byzantine exarch of Ceuta (Septem) opposite Gibraltar. If this is so, his comparative isolation explains what is tolerably certain—his close relations with one of the parties contending for the throne of the Visigothic kingdom of Spain. The legend tells how Julian became incensed because his beautiful daughter, who had been sent for her education to Toledo, the Visigothic capital, had been seduced by Roderick, who, whether usurper or not, was effectively but precariously king of Spain. In his rage Julian is said to have invoked Muslim help in order to gain his revenge. Apart from this story, a number of small indications suggest that Julian and the Visigothic opponents of Roderick deliberately tried to interest the Muslims in Spain and at first gave them considerable help.

About October 709 some of Julian's men are said to have made a raid across the straits and demonstrated to the Muslims that valuable booty was to be obtained. In July 710 a party of four hundred Muslims landed at the southernmost tip of Spain (west of Gibraltar) at the place now called Tarifa, after their leader, Ṭarīf. This reconnaissance in force was successful, and the Muslims were sufficiently confident to attempt a full-scale expedition in the following year. Seven thousand men were transported to near

Gibraltar in vessels provided by Julian. They were mostly Berbers, and their leader was a Berber client of Mūsā ibn-Nuṣayr (the Arab governor of north-west Africa) whose name Ṭāriq ibn-Ziyād has been perpetuated in *Gibraltar*, a corruption of "Jabal Ṭāriq", the mountain of Ṭāriq. Ṭāriq was a competent commander who had been placed in command of the forces garrisoning Tangier. Owing to the absence of King Roderick in the north the Muslims had time to establish a base on the site of the later town of Algeciras. Roderick hurried south, however, on receiving news of the expedition, and on 19 July attacked the Muslims in a valley or wadi, now generally identified with that of the Rio Barbate. The Muslims had been reinforced by a contingent of five thousand men, while some of Roderick's troops are said to have been disaffected and to have withdrawn from the battle. The result was a decisive victory for the Muslims. Roderick either was killed in battle or else he disappeared.

This victory demolished the central organisation of the Visigothic kingdom. There was further resistance, but only on a local or regional basis. Ṭāriq quickly realised that Spain was open to him, and made for Cordova first. On the way he defeated a pocket of Visigothic fugitives at Écija, and as a result gained the support of Jews and other discontented groups over a wide area. He thereupon decided to advance with the main army to the Visigothic capital, Toledo, which he apparently occupied without serious opposition. He was probably also able to make a reconnaissance to the north-east in the direction of Saragossa before settling down to winter in Toledo. Meanwhile, in October, Cordova surrendered to a detachment of seven hundred horsemen.

According to the sources, the provincial governor of north-west Africa, Mūsā ibn-Nuṣayr, was filled with jealousy on learning of Ṭāriq's successes, but this may be a distortion of the facts. His conduct is compatible with dispassionate planning to make the most of the opportunity which had been given to the Muslims. With eighteen thousand men, mostly Arabs, he crossed the straits in July 712 and advanced on Seville. Several smaller places were captured on the way, and resistance at Seville itself overcome. He then moved northwards against a strong remnant of Visigoths who withdrew into Mérida, and held out against the Muslim besiegers until June 713. It was apparently only after this that Mūsā and Ṭāriq met, the place being Talavera, a little way down the Tagus from Toledo. Apart from the quelling of a few revolts little is recorded during the year 713, but presumably the Muslim armies were busy consolidating their hold on the territory so far occupied.

During the following year Mūsā occupied Saragossa, and may have sent out exploratory probes which reached as far as Narbonne, for the Visigothic kingdom had included part of south-east France, including the Mediterranean littoral. He then seems to have decided that affairs in the west were more urgent and to have moved westwards and penetrated into the Asturias. Ṭāriq had already occupied Leon and Astorga, and Fortún of Aragon had submitted to him and become a Muslim. In the course of the year, however, Mūsā and Ṭāriq were summoned to the court of the caliph at Damascus. A fine story has been made of Mūsā's slow triumphal progress through North Africa and Egypt with a great train of captives and an unbelievably rich booty, and then of his harsh treatment by the caliph and his death in prison or at least in poverty; but here again much is legendary. Mūsā must have left Spain in the autumn of 714, for he reached Damascus probably in February 715.

In Spain the supreme command was left to Mūsā's son ʿAbd-al-ʿAzīz, who ably continued the work of occupying the country until he was assassinated in March 716. The Muslim hold on the north and north-east was extended by the capture of Pamplona near the western end of the Pyrenees and of Tarragona, Gerona and (probably) Narbonne on the Mediterranean seaboard. In the south-east Malaga and Elvira were taken, and a treaty made with prince Tudmīr (Theodemir) of Murcia. All these events presumably belong to 715, except that the treaty may have been in 713.

With the death of ʿAbd-al-ʿAzīz the phase of conquest and occupation may be reckoned as having come to an end. The whole of the Iberian peninsula had not been conquered nor occupied. In the north-west in particular there was a large area that was virtually untouched. Elsewhere, too, there were probably localities where Muslim control was not effective. Yet in essentials the organisational unity of the country, which had vanished in the break-up of Visigothic power, had been restored. There had been created a network of administration, with adequate military backing, covering nearly the whole peninsula, and the actual degree of control exercised by the central Muslim authority was probably greater than that of the later Visigothic kings.

(2)

THE PROVINCE OF THE DAMASCUS CALIPHATE

1. *The Organisation of the Province*

THE Arabs called their new domain in the Iberian peninsula "al-Andalus". The word is thought to be a corruption of "Vandalicia", a name derived from the Vandal invaders. It was used exclusively for that part of the peninsula under Muslim rule, so that, as the Reconquista progressed, the geographical area to which the term was applied contracted. In modern usage Andalusia is applied to that region of south-eastern Spain where the Moors had their last foothold in the thirteenth to fifteenth centuries.

For the Arabs al-Andalus was only a province, or part of a province, of a vast empire which stretched from al-Andalus and Morocco to Central Asia and the Punjab. The ruler of the empire was the caliph. This term is an adaption of the Arabic *khalīfa*, which means successor or deputy. The caliph was the man who had succeeded to the temporal but not the spiritual powers of Muḥammad. The first four successors of Muḥammad ruled from 632 to 661 and are known as "the rightly-guided caliphs" (*rāshidūn*). From 661 to 750 the caliphate was in the hands of the family of Umayya, a branch of the tribe of Quraysh which inhabited Mecca; some members of the family had been among the leading merchants of the town during Muḥammad's lifetime. The Umayyad caliphs had Damascus for their capital, though the court was often at one of their palaces elsewhere in Syria.

Despite the huge area controlled by the Umayyad caliphs, the organisation of government at the centre was still conceived along the lines of an Arabian nomadic tribe. Above all, it was concerned with persons rather than places. The caliph, too, was far from being an autocrat. On the analogy of a tribal shaykh he was expected to consult the leading men of his entourage, and in general to act towards them as first among equals. The weakness of such a system, in relation to the problems of a large empire, was not far to seek, and some of the later Umayyads tended towards the autocratic Persian tradition of statecraft—a tradition which was at the basis of the succeeding ʻAbbāsid régime. A matter of particular difficulty was that of succession to the office of caliph. According to Arab ideas, primogeniture gave no special privileges, and even the succession of son to father was not the only possibility. The new chief or shaykh of a tribe was usually the best fitted adult male from a certain family, agreed on in a meeting of the leading members of the tribe. Thus the retaining of the caliphate in the Umayyad family was not achieved without manipulation, and was felt by many Arabs to be a usurpation.

The caliphs, following the example of Muḥammad, delegated various duties to individuals. The most important position was that of general of an army. As wide territories came to be conquered, the generals assumed the role of provincial governors. The change, if such it can be called, was a very simple one. When an army retired to winter in a garrison-city in recently acquired land—in Cairouan, for example—the general continued in his command, which became virtually a civil one, since the only full citizens of the Islamic state were the soldiers under him. Financial and judicial matters usually came under separate officials, who might be appointed directly by the caliph; but the general-governor was the man in charge.

The non-Muslims in a province of the caliphate had, as

already noted, the status of "protected persons" or *dhimmīs* (though it is said that in al-Andalus *dhimmīs* was a word that came to be applied only to Jews). The existing local government was retained, and the head of each community became responsible to the Muslim authority for the payment of the tribute and other taxes and for the maintenance of internal order. In the Middle East this responsible man was usually the previous religious head of a religious group, such as a patriarch or bishop. This seems also to have been the normal case in Spain, but in 713 a treaty was made with Tudmīr (Theodemir), the prince of Murcia, confirming him in his rights as prince, and his subjects in—among other things—the practice of their religion. Where a community refused the first summons to surrender, and was then defeated in battle, the same status of "protected persons" was granted, but the conditions were liable to be more arduous and the amount of tribute and tax higher.

Originally, all the Muslim Arabs were liable to military service and all received stipends from the state. They thus constituted a superior military caste. When movable booty was captured on expeditions, it was usually sold to dealers and the proceeds divided among the participants in the expedition. Lands, however, were not sold, but left to the existing owners and tenants, and the rents paid into the central exchequer. Where the owners had fled, however—as was presumably the case with some of the Visigothic noble families—the governor of the province had the right to donate these lands to Muslims; so in course of time many of the Muslims became landowners. It is difficult to follow in detail the transition from a stipend-receiving class to a land-owning one in any part of the caliphate, and it is particularly difficult in Spain. By about 750 the system of paying stipends had apparently ceased to be important—presumably because it had come to be a relatively small part of a man's income—and it probably fell into desuetude soon after that. Before this happened, however, many Arabs in al-Andalus had become landowners, usually residing in towns close to their estates.

Until about 700 the non-Arabs in the heartlands of the caliphate were not encouraged to become Muslims. Sometimes, because of the loss of revenue resulting from conversions (since Muslims were not subject to the poll-tax), steps were taken to discourage them from leaving their religious communities. There was always greater readiness to receive those who were prepared to take part in military expeditions, and the presumption is that all the Berbers who entered Spain had become Muslims. Up to about 750, however, a non-Arab, in order to become a Muslim, had to become a client (*mawlā*, pl. *mawālī*) of an Arab tribe. This was apparently because the Islamic state was still regarded as a federation of Arab tribes. Since the status of client was felt to be an inferior one, and usually carried a smaller stipend than that of the pure Arabs, there was discontent among the non-Arab Muslims, who seem to have been increasing rapidly in numbers during the first half of the eighth century. This discontent was an important factor contributing to the fall of the Umayyad caliphate of Damascus. The necessity for non-Arab Muslims to become clients of Arab tribes seems to have quietly disappeared soon after 750. In al-Andalus the Berbers, who mostly came from the mountainous parts of North Africa, settled in similar terrain and made a living by pasturing animals.

While al-Andalus was part of the Damascus caliphate, its governors came under the Governor of Ifrīqiyya (Tunisia), stationed in Cairouan, and not directly under the caliph. This was a reasonable arrangement in view of the length of time taken for communications and travel. In the period from 716 to 756 about twenty men served as governor, some more than once. Only three held the position for five years or more. Some were only temporary governors, replacing men who had died in warfare against the Christians, or in other ways. Because they were so far from Damascus and even from Cairouan, they were largely independent (and this was doubtless one reason for the frequent changes). Like the caliphs, however, they were not autocratic, but had to show some regard for the opinion of the leading Arabs in al-Andalus. The last of the governors, Yūsuf ibn-ʿAbd-ar-Raḥman al-Fihrī, seems to have been appointed at an election in the province in 747. This was a time when the power of the caliph in Damascus was already crumbling away. Immediately after the conquest the provincial capital had been Seville (instead of the Visigoths' capital of Toledo), but about 717 it was transferred to Cordova, as being more central.

2. *The End of the Advance*

Since the Visigothic kingdom extended into southern France, it was natural for the Arabs to occupy this part, also, of the kingdom which they had conquered. It was indeed part of the vacuum they had created by destroying the central administration of the Visigoths. Unfortunately, information about the Muslim occupation of France and their expeditions there is scanty, but it is likely that, if there had been serious Visigothic resistance in France, some mention would have been made of it. The raids into the region of Narbonne may have begun soon after the defeat of the Visigoths in Spain. Certainly by 719 the Arab governor of the time, Samḥ, was able to occupy Narbonne and advance towards Toulouse. Energetic action by the duke of Aquitaine, Eudo, however, led in 721 to the repulse of the Muslims from Toulouse and the death of Samḥ.

This reverse did not prevent the Muslims from attempting to find other lines of advance into France. In 725 Carcassonne and Nîmes were occupied, and from there a force made its way northwards up the valley of the Rhône. It is said to have reached Autun on the Saône, or even further. This probing operation, however, does not seem to have been followed up. Instead there was an exploration of the route to the west of the Pyrenees by ʻAbd-ar-Raḥmān al-Ghāfiqī. He collected his troops at Pamplona in 732 and advanced into France by the pass of Roncesvalles. Eudo of Aquitaine was defeated and Bordeaux occupied. Then the Muslims pressed on northwards, making for Tours, where plentiful booty was to be expected. Eudo, however, alerted Charles Martel, the prince of the Franks, whose power had been growing and who at once realised the seriousness of the danger. He marched south to counter the Muslim threat, and between Tours and Poitiers, towards the end of October 732, there took place a battle, variously known as the battle of Tours and the battle of Poitiers. The Muslims were defeated and their leader killed. Some of the retreating force appears to have made for Narbonne. There is no record of the Muslims having again attempted to invade France by this western route.

Before considering the significance of the battle of Tours it will be useful to mention some pieces of information about events in the years immediately following. In 734 the Muslims showed renewed interest in the valley of the Rhône, and an expedition from Narbonne occupied Arles and Avignon. About 738, however, they were driven back by Charles Martel. He even advanced to Narbonne, and besieged it for a time; but he was unable to capture it. Nothing is heard of further activity in this region until after the fall of the Damascus caliphate. Then, most probably in 751 (though possibly not until 759) the successor of Charles Martel finally recaptured this important base from the Muslims.

The battle of Tours is often called one of the decisive battles of world history. Although in a sense it was, it would be more accurate to describe it as the point at which the tide turned. There was no cataclysmic destruction of

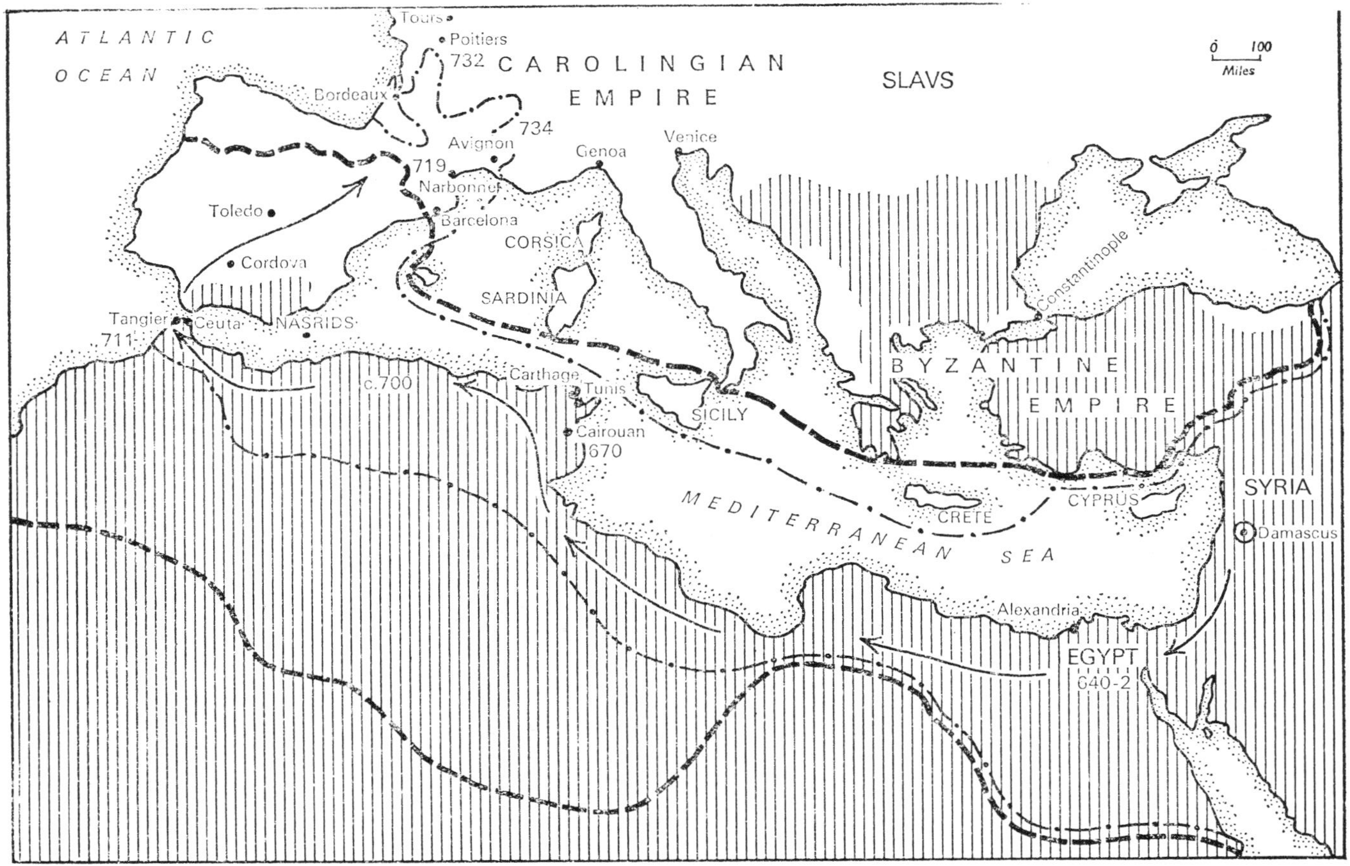

MAP I. Approx. boundaries Islamic influence, —·—·— early 8th c.; ▬ ▬ ▬ early 9th c.; ||||||| *c.* 1400.

the central military and political power of Muslim Spain. This continued much as it had been, but the leaders now realized that the route by the west of the Pyrenees was not a satisfactory line of expansion. The defeats by Charles Martel in 738 showed that expansion up the Rhône valley had also ceased to be either possible or desirable. All these expeditions into France, however, were thoroughly in keeping with the policy which had directed the Muslim advance through North Africa and into Spain. While the personal motives of some of the expeditionaries were religious, and while religious factors may have entered into the general strategy, the immediate aim of the expeditions was plunder. The Muslims were chiefly interested in regions where much plunder was to be had easily. They were prepared to fight, and to fight fiercely, but only to a limited extent. If advance in a certain direction meant serious and long-continued fighting, the plunder ceased to be worth the efforts required to gain it; and probing expeditions would be sent out in other directions. What the victory of Charles Martel at Tours showed was that his strength was now such that this line of advance had ceased to be lucrative; and his subsequent moves against Narbonne made it clear that advances into France no longer offered any hope of profit.

The matter could be put in another way, namely, that the Muslims' will to advance was weaker than the Franks' will to resist that advance; but various internal factors contributed to the weakening of the will to advance. Besides the increasing "cost" of the plunder, it has to be remembered that the Muslims, accustomed to a Mediterranean climate, may have found that of central France uncongenial. They doubtless also had some premonitions of the break-up of the Damascus caliphate, and for this reason felt insecure. Their available man-power, too, Arab and Berber, must already have been stretched to the utmost of its capacity. So for many reasons the Muslims had little desire to continue their attempts to advance into France. The tide had begun to ebb.

It was not only in France, however, that the tide turned. In north-west Spain also a Muslim recession began. Little is known about what was happening here in the quarter-century after 711. Presumably there were Muslim garrisons in all the towns of any size. Yet in strongholds in the mountains there were small groups who refused to submit. There were possibly Visigothic nobles among them, but the will to resist apparently came chiefly from the leaders of the local populations, and in the first place the Galicians,[1] since the whole outlook of these people was different from that of the Visigoths. A somewhat legendary story of how at Covadonga a Muslim force (accompanied by the metropolitan of Seville) was repulsed by prince Pelayo may be dated in 718 or between 721 and 726. Apart from this nothing is recorded until the reign of Alfonso I, king of the Asturias, 739–57. He reconquered much of north-west Spain and Portugal. The Muslims may have withdrawn from nearly a quarter of the Iberian peninsula, though not all of this was occupied by the followers of Alfonso. Some was left largely uninhabited to constitute the "marches".

The reasons for this turn of the tide in Spain itself were not unlike those for that in France. In addition there were some special factors contributing to the result. The Muslim settlers here were chiefly Berbers, and, as will presently be seen, they were dissatisfied with the way the Arabs treated them, and had risen in revolt. Then, beginning in 750, there was a serious famine which, coming on top of everything else, caused many of them to leave their Spanish lands and return to Africa.

The historian, especially the historian of Europe who is aware of the importance of the Reconquista in the emergence of Spain, sees in the successes of Alfonso I the seeds of the destruction of Muslim power in Spain; and in a sense this is so. From the Muslim point of view, however, what happened in this period of the collapse of the Damascus caliphate merely meant that al-Andalus was to have an untidy frontier; but it was no more untidy than many other frontiers of the caliphate, and the existence of the kingdom of the Asturias did not in itself mean that this realm of al-Andalus was doomed to extinction before it had well begun to live. It merely meant that the Muslims had constantly to face a challenge from the north. The real problem is why in the long run Christian strength grew and Muslim strength declined.

3. *Internal Tensions of the Province*

The rapid occupation of almost the whole Iberian peninsula together with the attempts at further expansion into France inevitably had repercussions among the agents of these operations, namely, the Arabs and their Berber allies. The conversion of the local inhabitants to Islam had begun before 750, but the numbers were not sufficient to constitute them a separate factor in the politics of the day.

Much of the tension which is found among the Arabs is ascribed, in the sources, to the rivalry between tribes and groups of tribes. In particular there was a bitter feud between two groups known as the Qaysites and the Kalbites, and this feud sometimes extended to larger groups genealogically connected with the original pair of tribes, until practically all the tribes of Arabia were involved. This rivalry between the tribes was over-emphasised by Dozy in his presentation of the history of Islamic Spain, and this has been recognised by his disciple Lévi-Provençal. Undoubtedly, however, tribal rivalry did exist and was a factor to be taken account of in politics. The difficulty is to know how to interpret it. Two aspects have to be distinguished: the significance of the facts at the centre of the caliphate, and their significance in al-Andalus.

In the caliphate in general the rivalry was usually between groups of tribes, and the Muslim historians justify and explain this by alleging that the groups which associated with one another were genealogically linked. Modern European historians, however, tend to regard the genealogies as subsequent to the groupings (that is, invented by genealogists of the Umayyad period); and the way in which the groupings vary in different regions is one confirmation of this. The actual groupings, too, appear to be derived from conditions in the garrison towns and conquered provinces and not from the pre-Islamic situation in Arabia. Instead of blaming ancient feuds, modern historians see the basis of the tension in Syria in the fact that many Kalbites had been settled there before the Arab expansion, whereas those who came with the expansion were mostly Qaysites. Thus there was a contemporary social and perhaps also economic difference underlying the tension.

After 740, tribal rivalry became an important political factor in al-Andalus. In part what happened in the province may simply have been a reflection of what was happening at the capital. The Qaysites and Kalbites functioned almost like parties in a modern state. While the caliph was relying mainly on one party, most of the provincial appointments went to its members. Social and economic differences between the two groups no doubt influenced their support of different policies; but the meagre sources do not appear to have been examined from this point of view.

Very little is known about what was happening to Spain between 720 and 740. Raiding expeditions were made into France; the pacification and settlement of the country continued; and local revolts were quelled. In 740, however, a revolt of Berbers broke out in North Africa, and Tangier was captured by the insurgents. Troops sent by the governor from his seat at Cairouan were defeated, and in 741, despite reinforcements of Syrians from Damascus, his army was again defeated. These successes led to a Berber revolt in the north-west of Spain. All the Berbers were thoroughly dissatisfied with the treatment which they received at the hands of the Arabs. They were given inferior shares of whatever was distributed, and the less desirable regions in which to settle, and, although they were Muslims, the Arabs did not regard them as equals. Since they were more numerous, and possibly also tougher fighters man for man, it was not surprising that they were initially successful.

Towards the end of 741, however, an important new element came upon the scene in al-Andalus. After the Berber victory in North Africa seven thousand horsemen of the Syrian reinforcements, under their leader Balj, took refuge in Ceuta and were besieged by the Berbers. In this somewhat difficult situation they agreed with the governor of al-Andalus that, if he supplied the transport, they would fight against the rebels in Spain and leave again when the rebellion was over. They were accordingly ferried across, and defeated three columns of Berbers one after the other, and would presumably have left had the governor not tried to evade carrying out his part of the agreement in full. This governor was of the Kalbite, or rather the wider Yemenite, party, while the Syrian Arabs under Balj were Qaysites. Instead of leaving the country, therefore, they marched on Cordova and expelled the governor, installing Balj in his place. The opposing Arabs reorganised themselves and gained some Berber support, but were defeated by Balj in August 742, though he himself was killed.

The new governor sent from Cairouan tried to quieten the country by settling the Syrians on lands in the valley of the Guadalquivir and along the south coast. In Syria they had been *jundīs*, that is, men who received fiefs of land in return for being ready to serve in the army when required; and their settlement in al-Andalus was on similar terms. This did not prevent them combining with certain other

Arab tribes and from 745 to 755 maintaining in power governors favourable to their interests. By 755 the opposing Yemenite Arabs were showing signs of preparing to challenge the dominant coalition, while the north of the country was recovering from the famine which had afflicted it since 750. At this juncture ʿAbd-ar-Raḥmān (born 730), a young member of the Umayyad family, who had escaped from Iraq and Syria when all his relatives had been annihilated by the ʿAbbāsids on their coming to power in 750, despatched an emissary to al-Andalus. ʿAbd-ar-Raḥmān had lived for some time with his Berber mother's tribe near the Mediterranean coast of Morocco, and his emissary was enthusiastically received by some of the Syrian *jundīs*, who were mostly clients of the Umayyads. The leaders of the group in power since 745 at first hesitated and finally rejected ʿAbd-ar-Raḥmān's proposals. Upon this the emissary successfully approached the opposing Yemenite group. ʿAbd-ar-Raḥmān crossed the straits, and with an army of Syrian *jundīs*, Yemenites and some Andalusian Berbers defeated the remnants of the Qaysite group in May 756. The country as a whole then submitted to him, and he was proclaimed emir of al-Andalus in the mosque of Cordova. The Umayyad emirate had been established.

(3)

THE INDEPENDENT UMAYYAD EMĪRATE

1. *The Establishment of the Emirate*

'Abd-ar-Raḥmān I : 756–788
Hishām I : 788–796
al-Ḥakam I : 796–822
'Abd-ar-Raḥmān II : 822–852

THE proclamation of 'Abd-ar-Raḥmān as emir created a novel situation, though the novelty was more theoretical than practical. The title of "emir" or "commander" had hitherto been used by provincial governors appointed by the caliph; but, since the 'Abbāsid caliphs were responsible for the massacre of nearly all the Umayyad family, there could be no question of 'Abd-ar-Raḥmān recognising the caliph in any way. On the other hand, his position was never such that he could claim the office of caliph for himself. So, for the first time in the Islamic world, there was a political entity which, without justifying itself by heretical dogma, was organised in complete independence of the main body of Muslims. This was the theoretical novelty.

In practice, however, the element of novelty was not great. When communications stretched over vast distances and were slow, provincial governors were largely left to their own devices. This had been particularly the case in the last decade or so before the fall of the Umayyad caliphate in 750. The caliph had indeed sent a large force from Syria to help against the Berber revolt in North Africa.

Although from this force the horsemen under Balj had crossed into Spain, this had been a more or less private arrangement between the governor and the men concerned; and after this event the Muslims in al-Andalus had been almost entirely on their own. The chief novelty in ʿAbd-ar-Raḥmān's position, then, was that he had no superior to call on him to demit office, and that he had a certain right to rule. Perhaps also the knowledge that al-Andalus was thus isolated emboldened rebels in their attempts to seize power. The possibility that the ʿAbbāsids might try to assert their authority over this part of the empire of their predecessors had also to be taken into account; but it cost them much time and effort to secure even a tenuous hold over North Africa, and they were never a serious threat to the new Umayyad régime in Spain.

The main problem with which ʿAbd-ar-Raḥmān and his immediate successors had to cope, in order to establish the emirate securely, was the diversity of elements, mainly racial, in the population. First of all came the Arabs who, though not numerous, held a dominant position; and they were further divided among themselves. The old opposition, however, between Yemenites (or Kalbites) and Qaysites seems gradually to have merged into another, namely, that between Arabs of the first wave, known as "old-established" (*baladiyyūn*), and the later comers, known as "Syrians" (*shāmiyyūn*). Since the Syrians, as explained above, had been given fiefs, this distinction was in part a social and economic one. The Arabs, of course, were all Muslims.

In addition there were two other groups of Muslims, the Berbers and the local converts. The Berbers were much the more numerous, for they had supplied the bulk of the invading and occupying man-power. The more significant of the Berber immigrants were those from the sedentaries (as distinct from the nomads), and in Spain they turned again to agricultural activity. Despite their numbers they were, as we have noted, treated as inferiors by the Arabs, and discontent constantly smouldered among them. The local converts, it would seem, came, after a time, to be as numerous as the Berbers, or even more so. The term for "convert" was *musālim*, but this seems to have been restricted to those who actually *changed* their religion. The normal name among the Arabs for Spanish Muslims was *muwalladūn*, which might be rendered "born Muslims". They are usually referred to by Spanish writers as "renegades", a term which doubtless was not used until the Reconquista was well under way. The chief motive for the acceptance of Islam by a large section of the Spanish population was probably its association with a higher and very attractive civilisation, coupled with distrust of the Christian bishops because of their close identification with the unpopular Visigothic rule.

The remaining large element in the Islamic state—the Christian population who kept their religion—were called Mozarabs (*musta'ribūn*), which might be rendered "arabizers", again probably a later term used by the Christians of the Reconquista.[1] Though Christian, these people also were presumably attracted by many aspects of Arab and Islamic civilisation. They were by no means hostile to Muslim rule, but learnt Arabic (though they also spoke a Romance dialect[2]) and adopted many Arab customs. Besides the Christians there were many Jews in the chief towns, who, having suffered under the Visigoths, actively aided the Muslim conquest, and do not appear later to have thought of revolting.

With all these diverse and often discordant elements, even to maintain effective rule was difficult. There were numerous revolts and risings of one kind or another. Sometimes only one of the groups mentioned was involved;

PLATE I. Door and blind arches in the western façade of the mosque at Cordova, showing tile and bas-relief decoration characteristic of the art of the Caliphate.

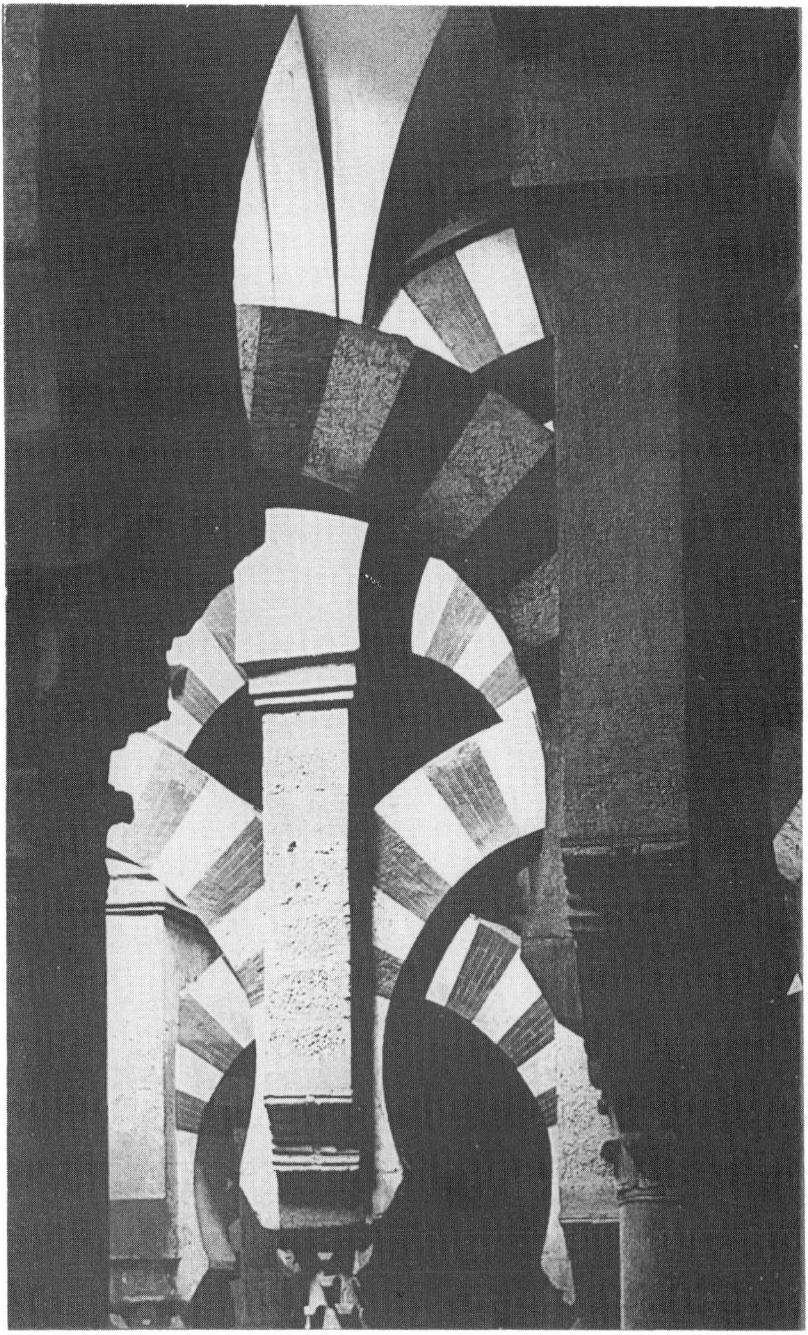

sometimes two or more would join together. The old system by which every able-bodied Muslim was liable for service had broken down before 750, and would in any case have been of little use in dealing with the situation in al-Andalus. One of ʿAbd-ar-Raḥmān's methods of tackling the problem was to create a professional army. This probably consisted largely of slaves, who were easily obtainable from north of the Pyrenees. The size of this mercenary army was increased by his successors. This made the emir independent of his subjects, but it also created serious problems for him.

It has been suggested that the Umayyads achieved unity from this heterogeneous body by identifying their cause with that of Islam, but there are complexities which this suggestion does not explain. The matter will be considered more fully in a later chapter. Here let it be noted that this was at best a long-term policy. For the moment the aim was to make the emir the centre of unity, but to begin with his authority could only be maintained by sheer force. A notorious example of this is the so-called "day of the Foss" at Toledo, probably in 797 (not in 807) soon after al-Ḥakam began to rule. All the notables of Toledo, mainly Spanish Muslims, who had earlier shown signs of disaffection, were tricked by the governor into entering the castle on the pretext of paying their respects to the heir to the throne; once inside they were beheaded one by one and the bodies thrown into a trench or foss.

Towards the end of the same reign, probably in 818, there was an even more notorious blood-bath at Cordova. The harshness of the emir provoked a rising among the inhabitants of the "suburb" south of the Guadalquivir. For a time the issue was in doubt, but eventually the emir's troops gained the upper hand; the "suburb" was plundered,

---

PLATE 2. Red and white striped arches of the mosque at Cordova.

three hundred of the leading survivors were executed, the rest of the people made to leave Cordova, and the whole of the "suburb" ploughed up. The importance attached to these events in the Arabic sources and in some older European accounts should not make the modern reader suppose that there was nothing besides force to support the central authority. In the revolt of the "suburb" one or two Muslim jurists were involved, and this appearance of a new class is at the same time an indication that the Umayyads were trying to develop justice and fair treatment in their realm.

While the Umayyads were thus busy establishing their rule throughout the territories that had come into their hands, there were no events of primary importance on the northern frontier, though there was a certain amount of activity. In the years from 740 to 755 the little kingdom of the Asturias in the north-west of the Iberian peninsula was able to expand somewhat and to make itself relatively secure against attacks. Beyond the Pyrenees, again, Charlemagne (771–814) was building his powerful empire. Occasionally he made incursions into the peninsula, as in 801 when he entered Barcelona. His expedition of 778 against Saragossa has been made famous by the *Chanson de Roland*. The central event in this poem, the defeat of a rearguard at Roncesvalles, was a very minor affair from the military standpoint; but the more important aspect of the campaign—the failure to take Saragossa—may have influenced Charlemagne to leave Spain alone for the most part.

Al-Andalus had no northern frontier in the modern sense. Between the area securely held by the Muslims and that securely held by the various Christian states was a tract of land more loosely held and merging into a no-man's land. These were the Marches. The Muslim defence was based on Saragossa for the Upper March, on Toledo for the Middle March, and on Mérida for the Lower March. At certain periods the Muslims made an expedition northwards every summer, but these periods alternated with periods of apparent truce. One of the most notable expeditions was to Narbonne in 793, and there was another in 841 to the same neighbourhood. Neither the latter nor one in 828 explicitly against Barcelona was able to recapture that town from the Franks.

By the reign of ʿAbd-ar-Raḥmān II (822–52) the Umayyad emirate was well established, and the country was prospering. There were still revolts, but they were peripheral, while at the centre a measure of unity had been achieved. One index of the general prosperity was the extensive building programme carried out by ʿAbd-ar-Raḥmān II. The series of watch-posts set up after 844 to guard against Norse sea-raiders shows the strength and practical efficiency of the régime. Indeed, ʿAbd-ar-Raḥmān II felt sufficiently powerful to enter into the politics of the various small and middle-size states which occupied the region from Morocco to Tunisia, and to support some of the smaller ones against their larger neighbours. A full discussion, however, of the basis of Umayyad power and prosperity will best come after we have seen the state at its zenith in the next century.

2. *The Crisis of the Emirate*

Muḥammad I : 852–886
al-Mundhir : 886–888
ʿAbd-Allāh : 888–912

When ʿAbd-ar-Raḥmān II died in 852, the Umayyad state was prospering, and appeared to be strong and securely established. Yet the events of the next sixty years showed that this appearance was deceptive, and that in reality the structure was fragile and precarious. The troubles in the earlier period had nearly all been due to townsmen who were discontented for one reason or another, and who had to vent their discontent by hitting out at authority; at the same time they had little idea of a genuine alternative to the existing régime and political system. Before the end of the ninth century, however, there had appeared a number of ambitious individuals who found in popular discontent an instrument by which they could create an independent or semi-independent little state for themselves.

This feature seems to have begun in the Marches. The general conception of the Marches was good, and proved an effective means of defending the more densely populated parts of the country in the south and south-east. The system, however, implied giving a measure of power and independence to the governors of the Marches and various subordinate lords. As early as 842 one of the latter, Mūsā ibn-Mūsā ibn-al-Qasī, governor of Tudela, refused to obey the emir, and successfully resisted a series of attacks by the emir's troops. The emir eventually accepted his profession of loyalty, though on Mūsā's own terms. Before his death in 862 Mūsā was the effective ruler of most of the Upper March, including Saragossa, and even called himself "the third king of Spain". Beginning in 871 three of his sons, who retained most of the family possessions, attempted to regain his power, but the difficulties were too great, and in 884 the sole survivor sold Saragossa to the emir. The latter was not much better off, however, since he had to lean heavily in this region on a rival family of Arab origin often known as the Tujībids, who also demanded a measure of independence.

Two other not dissimilar series of events may be mentioned briefly. In the first case the *muwallad* (or Spanish Muslim) Ibn-al-Jillīqī maintained himself in partial independence in the region of Mérida in the Lower March from 875 onwards, and his sons and lieutenants did not fully submit to the central government until 930. In Seville, on the other hand, two Arab families gained the upper hand in a struggle with the *muwallads*, and then in 899, after a quarrel between them, the head of one became semi-independent ruler of the region, recognised by the emir and eventually succeeded by his sons.

The most threatening of these attempts at independence, however, was that of Ibn-Ḥafṣūn, another *muwallad*. In 880, with a company of malcontents, he raised a revolt in the south, making his centre the castle of Bobastro. The country was seething with discontent, and he had little difficulty in building up his own power and defying the Umayyad armies. With his successes his ambitions grew, and he allowed no principles to stand in the way of his efforts to increase his power. About 890 he was negotiating with the semi-independent ruler of Cairouan (recognized by the ʿAbbāsids) in order to obtain military support and become emir of Spain. At this period Ibn-Ḥafṣūn had much support from the *muwallads* who had gone over to him after being involved in fighting with the Arabs of the region. In 899, however, he may have lost much of this support by becoming a Christian, though he doubtless also gained much from the Mozarabs. This change of religion did not prevent him in 910 from professing his friendship for the Fāṭimid régime which had established itself in Tunisia in the previous year. Even under ʿAbd-ar-Raḥmān III the central government, though it weakened Ibn-Ḥafṣūn's power, was unable to dislodge him from Bobastro; and after his death in 917 his sons kept up their resistance for some ten years. The length of this insurrection is a clear index of the relative weakness of the central government.

One noteworthy feature of these events and of the period in general is the mingling of Christianity and Islam. The family of Mūsā ibn-Mūsā ibn-al-Qasī, in the Upper March, had ties of blood and marriage with the family which, at this same period, was creating the kingdom of Navarre round Pamplona; indeed it made contributions to the growth of that kingdom which were far from negligible. This point is probably to be connected with the spread of

Frankish feudal practices, since feudalism placed the emphasis on a man's relation to his lord to such an extent that his religion almost ceased to be relevant.[3] Many incidents of this period in which men changed religion or swore allegiance to a lord of the other religion suggest that these ninth-century struggles were not regarded primarily as struggles between the two religions. It would follow from this that, till this period, it cannot have been the policy of the Umayyads to make Islam the chief integrating force in al-Andalus, or at least, if they had such a policy, it had not so far become effective. On the other hand, the Umayyads may have been beginning to be interested in islamisation, for the emir ʿAbd-Allāh (888–912) is said to have been under the influence of the jurists, and the existence of jurists would be a mark of islamisation.

It is relevant at this point to mention the theory of Américo Castro in *The Structure of Spanish History* (130–170). He sees the cult of Saint James of Compostella, including the pilgrimages, as incorporating an old Galician or Iberian belief in the Heavenly Twins (since James was regarded as the twin-brother of Jesus), and also as giving the Galicians and their neighbours from the ninth century onwards the firm conviction that they had divine help in their war with the Muslims and that thereby they would eventually be victorious. This cult is therefore the source of the spiritual strength underlying the Reconquista. Apart from the theory it is certain that the cult existed in the first half of the ninth century, and that under Alfonso III (866–910), while the Muslims were busied with their internal divisions, the joint Asturian-Leonese kingdom expanded and grew stronger.

(4)

THE GRANDEUR OF THE UMAYYAD CALIPHATE

1. *Umayyad Spain at its Zenith*

'Abd-ar-Raḥmān III : 912–961
al-Ḥakam II : 961–976

THE emir 'Abd-Allāh was succeeded by his grandson 'Abd ar-Raḥmān III, a young man of twenty-one. When the new ruler came to the throne the prospects for al-Andalus were not bright. In addition to what was practically a civil war against Ibn-Ḥafṣūn, and to the diminishing control by the central government over the lords of the Marches, there were two external dangers appearing on the horizon: in the North, the kingdom of Leon and, in what is now Tunisia, the new Fāṭimid power. Yet by his gifts of character and statesmanship and by the good fortune of a long reign 'Abd-ar-Raḥmān was able not merely to overcome these weaknesses and threats, but also to bring al-Andalus to a height of greatness.

One of his prime concerns was the restoration of internal unity. Vigorous and well-conducted campaigns during the first two years of his reign led to the defeat of many supporters of Ibn-Ḥafṣūn in the outer section of his sphere of influence; to the reconciliation of waverers with the government in Cordova; and to the encouragement of those loyal to it. A large number of castles and strongholds were placed in reliable hands. Advantage was taken of a dispute within the family ruling Seville in only nominal dependence, and before the end of 913 a governor obedient to

ʿAbd-ar-Raḥmān had been installed. By such tactics Ibn-Ḥafṣūn's authority was greatly weakened, and after his death in 917 his sons quarrelled and their power disintegrated. The surrender of Bobastro in 928 marked the end of the threat to unity. In the years immediately following, ʿAbd-ar-Raḥmān completed the work of establishing effective control over the Marches. In the lower March this was marked by the surrender to him, in 930, of Badajoz, by a descendant of Ibn-al-Jillīqī. In the middle March it required a two-year siege before Toledo surrendered in 932. In the upper March, on the other hand, the Tujībids had from the first shown themselves relatively faithful vassals of ʿAbd-ar-Raḥmān, though in 937 the lord of Saragossa transferred his allegiance to the king of Leon, and it was only after a military campaign in the region and a siege of Saragossa that ʿAbd-ar-Raḥmān restored his control of the upper March.

Whilst the first twenty years of the reign thus saw the unity of al-Andalus re-established, they were also noteworthy for a large measure of success against the Christian kingdoms of the north, Leon and Navarre. It may be that the weakness of these states was in some way a repercussion of the collapse of the Carolingian empire, or it may be that the rulers of the period were less capable than some of their predecessors and successors. Certainly by expeditions in 920 and 924 ʿAbd-ar-Raḥmān was able to put a stop to the Christian raids into Muslim territory. A halt was placed to the extension of Muslim influence, however, during the reign of Ramiro II of Leon from 932 to 950. (It is convenient to speak simply of "Leon" for what is properly the kingdom of the Asturias and Leon.)

The climax of the successes of Ramiro was in 939. ʿAbd-ar-Raḥmān had marched against Leon with a larger army than usual, allegedly about a hundred thousand men. He was met by Ramiro at Simancas, just south of modern Valladolid. After several days of preliminary encounters the unwieldy Muslim forces were put to flight, and many lost their lives owing to the fact that Ramiro had previously dug a trench (*khandaq*) at their rear. This military disaster was not irreparable, but it was a severe blow to ʿAbd-ar-Raḥmān's pride. Ramiro took advantage of his success to resettle Christians in the neighbourhood of Salamanca. Presently, however, he became fully occupied in quelling the attempted assertion of its independence by Castile; and ʿAbd-ar-Raḥmān soon restored his military strength and his political influence.

After the death of Ramiro II in 950 internal disputes greatly weakened the Christian states, and the years from 951 to 961 witnessed a great increase in the power and influence of ʿAbd-ar-Raḥmān. The suzerainty or hegemony of ʿAbd-ar-Raḥmān and his successors was acknowledged by the king of Leon, the queen of Navarre and the counts of Castile and Barcelona; and this acknowledgement was no mere formal affair, but was accompanied by the payment of an annual indemnity or tribute; and failure to pay resulted in a punitive raid. At the same time a number of strongholds were dismantled or handed over to the Muslims. Thus from about 960 to the end of the century Muslim control of the Iberian peninsula was more complete than at any other time before or after.

This makes it pertinent to consider the view expressed by Arnold Toynbee in *A Study of History* (viii. 351) that the failure of ʿAbd-ar-Raḥmān and al-Manṣūr to complete the conquest of the peninsula at this period when they had undoubted military supremacy marked the turning of the tide—the end of Muslim expansion in this direction and the beginning of Christian recovery. A discussion of the point will throw into relief some important features of Umayyad Spain. In one sense the conquest of the peninsula was complete, for all the north-west corner was included in the kingdom of Leon, and Leon had acknowledged the suzerainty of ʿAbd-ar-Raḥmān. Yet the conquest was incomplete in two respects: no Muslims wanted to settle in these northern lands; and the local rulers remained vassals of a suzerain and did not become heads of communities of *dhimmīs* or "protected persons".

The reasons for the non-settlement of the northern lands are similar to those suggested above (pp. 22-26) for the lack of enthusiasm for the continued penetration of France after the defeat of 732, and for the failure to maintain pressure on the north-west about the middle of the eighth century. The Arabs almost certainly disliked the climate; and most of them were town-dwellers, who found the towns of the north small and lacking in comfort. It has been suggested that the Arabs were never happy except where olive-trees flourished. The Berbers who had originally settled in parts of the north-west had had unfortunate experiences before they withdrew, and this was doubtless remembered. The hardness of the life, coupled with the hostility of the local inhabitants, especially the mountaineers, made settlement in this region an unattractive proposition. Where lands were unoccupied or sparsely populated, it was rather the Christians who were prepared to undergo the rigours of resettlement.

The treatment of dependent political units in a feudal-like rather than a traditional Islamic manner might be explained by stating that the Muslims were only strong enough to impose a form of vassalage and not the complete Islamic *dhimmī*-status; but it is by no means clear that this supposition is justified. It is more likely that at many points traditional Arab and Islamic ideas were proving less satisfactory than local Spanish ideas in dealing with the peculiar problems of the northern frontier of al-Andalus. The conception of the holy war or *jihād*,[1] as already noted, was excellent for unifying the tribes of Arabia and directing their energies into the vast expansion of the first Islamic century; but even in the east this conception was not suited to be the guiding principle of a great empire in its policies with regard to its neighbours. In the west the problems had been intensified by the divisions among the Muslims of North Africa.

ʿAbd-ar-Raḥmān certainly made use of the idea of the holy war in summoning men to join the army, but for most of his soldiers the primary motive was probably materialistic and not religious. The existence of strategic castles naturally gave a special importance to the relation of the owner of such a castle to his liege-lord; and Islamic political tradition, which was concerned rather with the relation of political communities to one another, had nothing to say on this point. When it is further remembered that many of the leading *muwallads* or Spanish Muslims had close ties of kinship with some of the Christian noble families, it is not surprising that lords of castles often stood in relationships to one another which were conceived in purely feudal terms without regard for religion. In short, there had been a failure to adapt the distinctive Islamic political ideas to a situation where, largely for geographical reasons, castles and knights were the chief feature. This failure might conceivably be explained as due to a lack of religious fervour; but it would be more realistic to admit that, although Islam is said to be a political religion, Muslim rulers after the early days have mainly disregarded religious precepts in their conduct of politics. There is a certain autonomy about the wielding of political power, and for most rulers *raison d'état* outweighs all other considerations. It was only to be expected that Muslim rulers in the Western Europe of the tenth century should adopt the principles and practices which had been found politically effective there.

In considering ʿAbd-ar-Raḥmān's North African policy the major fact to be kept in mind is the establishment of the Fāṭimid dynasty first in 909 in Tunisia and then in 969 in Egypt. From one point of view this was the triumph of the sedentary Berbers over the nomads, whereas the earlier Arab conquest had been a victory of the nomads with the support of the Arabs over the sedentary tribes. Yet this was not the whole of the story. The Fāṭimid military and political successes were linked with the proclamation of a novel set of religious ideas. Preached by an enthusiastic agent (*dā'ī*) these ideas could win the active support of many simple men with the makings of good soldiers. Theologically the set of ideas is described as the Ismā'īlite form of Shī'ism.[2] It declared that the Islamic community had an appointed leader or imām—in the Tunisian case one 'Ubayd-Allāh—who was a descendant of Muḥammad and, as true imām, was divinely inspired and supported. The political implication was the overthrow of existing rulers (since they were not the rightful leaders of the community of Muslims) and their replacement by an autocratic administration under the true imām. In the particular case of the Fāṭimids, from the time they began to rule in Cairouan they took the claim to universal sovereignty in the Islamic world more seriously than others who had made similar claims before them. Agents were sent into most parts of the 'Abbāsid empire and skilfully turned local discontents into support for the Fāṭimids.

Much of the discontent with which Spain was then seething might thus have been turned to account by the Fāṭimids. The opportunism of Ibn-Ḥafṣūn, too, had led him to profess allegiance to the Fāṭimids on their attainment of power, and thereby to direct their attention towards Spain. Most of the Berber settlers were from sedentary tribes and might be expected to welcome religious ideas similar to those favoured by the Berber followers of the Fāṭimids. An incident in the middle March of al-Andalus in 901 had given an ominous warning of potentialities of this kind. Berber malcontents had rallied round a man claiming to be the Mahdī, the divinely guided imām, and he had led them against Zamora, which had recently been resettled by Christians; there he was defeated by the king of Leon and the movement died away. In such matters race or tradition appears to have counted for much. Interest in holy men was a normal feature of the religious life of the Berbers of North Africa, but it would appear that Iberians were more interested in knowing that supernatural powers not embodied in particular persons were working on their behalf. Américo Castro contrasts the French and English belief that the touch of a Christian king could cure scrofula with the Spanish belief in the "tangible, nearby power" of Santiago which gave men victory in battle—a power that was not incarnate in persons, but might operate through inanimate objects.[3] In so far as this was the case with the Spanish Muslims there was no real threat to al-Andalus from Fāṭimid propaganda; but this would not be clear to 'Abd-ar-Raḥmān III.

The pattern of events in North Africa was not very different from that on the northern frontiers. There was first of all a period of expansion when several small principalities accepted Umayyad suzerainty; by 931, after some military successes, most of the region from Algiers to Sijilmāsa recognised 'Abd-ar-Raḥmān as suzerain. Soon after this, however, his attention was distracted from North Africa by the aggressive policy of Ramiro II of Leon; and not long after the latter's death the Fāṭimid al-Mu'izz (953–975) began to work vigorously for expansion. After an expedition in 959 under his general Jaw'har only Tangier and Ceuta were left to 'Abd-ar-Raḥmān. So things remained until towards the end of the reign of al-Ḥakam II (961–76). Al-Mu'izz decided to concentrate his energies on eastward expansion. Egypt was conquered in 969 and the seat of government moved there in 972. From this time on Fāṭimid influence declined in the region from Tunisia to Morocco. Expeditions by the Umayyad general Ghālib in North Africa in 973 and 974 recovered some of the lost ground, and the Umayyads retained an important stake in North Africa until their central power began to decline.

The most important single event in the internal history of al-Andalus under ʿAbd-ar-Raḥmān III was linked with the threat from the Fāṭimids. This event was the assumption by that ruler in 929 of the titles of "caliph" (*khalīfa*) and "commander of the believers" (*amīr al-muʾminīn*), together with the "throne-name" of an-Nāṣir li-dīn-Allāh ("defender of the religion of God"). In making this claim what was asserted was not a universal right to rule all Muslims but the independence of the ruler of al-Andalus of all higher Muslim political authority. To support the claim he could point to his descent from the caliphs of Damascus; even before this the Spanish Umayyads had called themselves "the sons of the caliphs". The claim was thus not directed against the ʿAbbāsids but was to counter the claim of the Fāṭimids, and to give the petty rulers of North Africa some theological justification for recognising the suzerainty of the Umayyads of Cordova.

The increase of dignity deriving from this title was also appropriate in view of the success of ʿAbd-ar-Raḥmān's policies. The heightening of the separation between the ruler and the subjects, however, was probably not due to the assumption of the title of caliph, but to his general success and prosperity. Sheer pressure of administration would contribute to the change, just as it had forced some of the later Umayyad caliphs of Damascus to think of modelling themselves in part on Persian imperialism. It is thus not surprising that in the last years of his reign ʿAbd-ar-Raḥmān III is said to have been more autocratic.

Little need be said about the reign of ʿAbd-ar-Raḥmān's son, al-Ḥakam II (961–76), with the throne-name of Al-Mustanṣir bi-'llāh. The structure of centralised power created by his father remained intact, and so both internally and externally the situation of al-Andalus continued to be much as it had been. An attempt by the kingdoms of Leon, Castile and Navarre to assert their independence was defeated by an army under Ghālib in 975—the same general

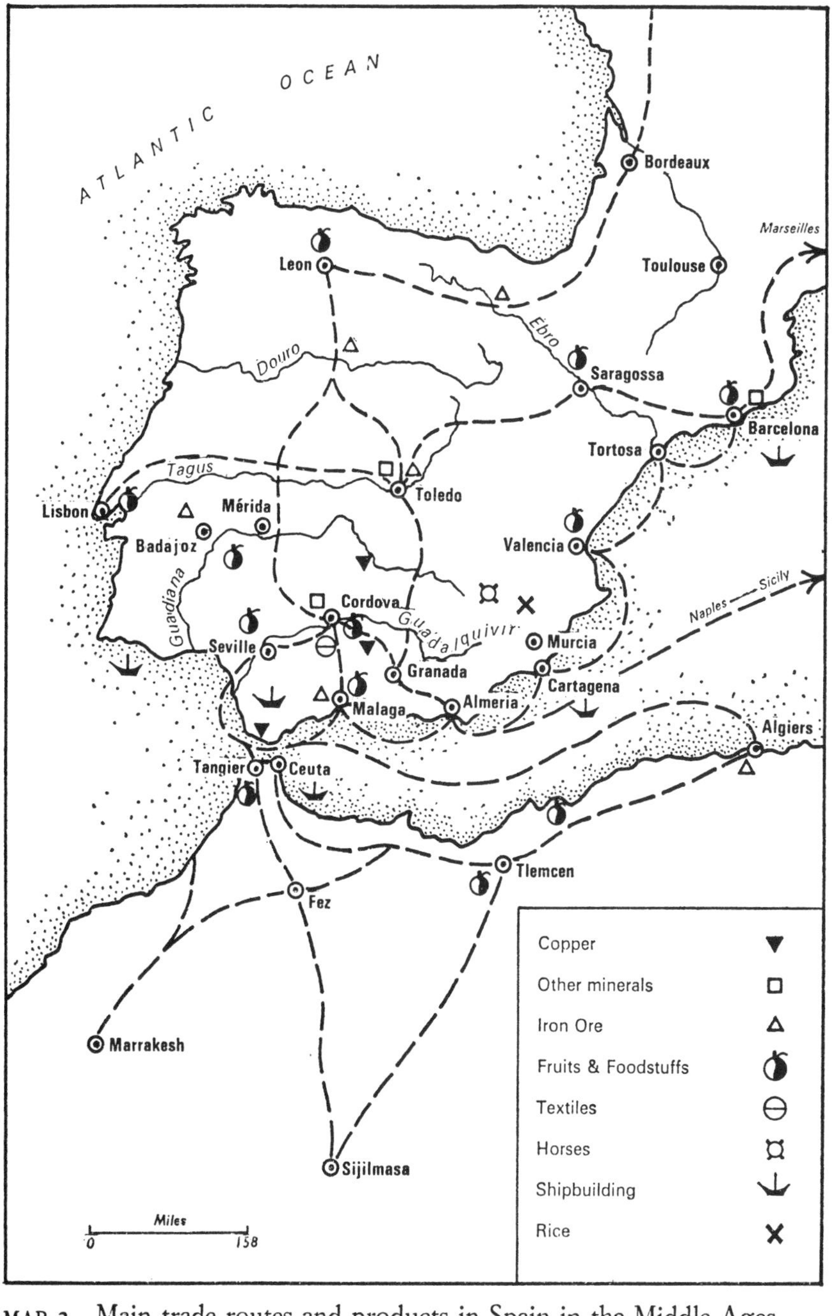

MAP 2. Main trade routes and products in Spain in the Middle Ages

who, as already noted, had begun to restore Umayyad influence in North Africa. In internal affairs the jurists appear to have become more important, but the whole question of the jurists is difficult and will have to be looked at more fully later. When al-Ḥakam II died in 976 the power of the Umayyad dynasty and the prosperity of their kingdom were still at their zenith, and there was little to presage the sudden decline after the year 1000.

2. *The Economic Basis*

After this brief description of the more obvious events of the reigns of ʿAbd-ar-Raḥmān III and his son, it is time to look at some of the broader questions raised. Above all, it has to be asked: what made this period a "great age"? When we admire it what are we admiring? Is it the concentration of political authority and wealth? Is it the fine buildings? Or is it something beyond these—perhaps an upsurge of the human spirit deriving from the prosperity and expressing itself in the art and architecture and literature? These are not questions that can be easily answered. Indeed it is part of the aim of this book to raise such questions and leave them unanswered; and the questions just indicated will be in the background for most of the rest of our study of Islamic Spain. At the moment, however, we turn to look at one particular point—the material basis of the prosperity of the Umayyad caliphate.

The agriculture of al-Andalus was nearly all of the "dry" type. This was all that was possible in the central plateau. In the south, however, in what is now Andalusia, irrigation was possible. This was not an Arab invention, but it seems to have been greatly developed by the Muslims, and they may have introduced improved techniques from the east.

PLATE 3. Stone lattice and foiled arch in the mosque at Cordova with characteristic arabesques of stylized floral motifs.

With a higher level of technical skill fresh crops became possible, and the Muslims are credited with bringing to Spain not only oranges and several other species of fruits and vegetables, but also rice, sugar-cane and cotton. Agriculturally al-Andalus was more prosperous than most other Islamic lands. It was also rich in minerals, and the Roman processes for obtaining these were probably continued. Certainly Muslim Spain inherited from the Visigoths notable techniques for artistic metal-work, and something of this seems to have been carried over to the present time.

It would seem, however, that the special contribution of Islam must be looked for rather in the sphere of urbanisation—in the development of towns and in what took place in them. Islam has always been primarily a religion of the townsman and not of the peasant. It grew up in Mecca, which was a thriving commercial and financial centre; though the caravans of the Meccan merchants went through the deserts or steppes of Arabia, the religion had little to do with the desert, and the desert-dwellers have seldom been the most zealous Muslims. It has, if possible, even less to do with the peasant. One indication of this is the standard Islamic calendar of twelve lunar months or 354 days—a calendar which no peasant religion would tolerate for a single year.

There had been a decline in municipal life in the sixth century under the Visigoths, and there had appeared a class of owners of large estates, in whose hands lay most of the power and influence in the country. The arrival of the Arabs with their wide experience of municipal administration in the east led to a partial reversal of the process, in that there was a gradual revival of town life. Though they had little in the way of democratic institutions, the Arabs seem to have encouraged a genuine feeling of citizenship.

PLATE 4. Arches in one of the main halls, possibly the throne room, at the Palace of Madīnat az-Zahrā'.

Order was strictly maintained. There were officials who looked after the markets and saw that there were no unfair practices. There were corporations or gilds of artisans, with grades equivalent to master, journeyman and apprentice, and these were carefully regulated. There were inns to give convenient accommodation to travelling merchants and their goods. Thus there were sound material or economic reasons for the growth of towns; and the Muslims were by no means unaware of the opportunities offered by towns for the cultivation of literature, music and other artistic and intellectual activities.

The stimulation of commerce resulting from the general Islamic ethos may well have been the chief source of the prosperity of al-Andalus. Not merely did the merchants use the land routes of the Iberian peninsula and penetrate into France (through which there was an extensive trade in slaves), but they almost certainly developed greatly the links which the Visigoths already had with North Africa. The precise importance of the relationship to North Africa, which has been emphasised by Lévi-Provençal, is not altogether clear, and is worthy of further study. In the ninth and tenth centuries the danger from the Norman sea-raiders led to the creation of a fleet, and as a repercussion of this a merchant marine grew up, which gave direct communications with Tunisia and Egypt; ships from these countries also shared in the traffic.

The urban industries naturally catered chiefly for the needs of the local population, but, as the townsmen prospered and commerce increased, there was also a market at home and abroad for luxury goods. The inherited skills and techniques were employed, and fresh ones elaborated. Al-Andalus became noted for its magnificent textiles; and it also produced furs and ceramic objects.

It is interesting to note that this general picture of Muslim economic influences in Spain is confirmed by a study of Arabic words in modern Spanish. There is a large number of such words, but the important point is to notice the spheres of life to which they belong. Very many are connected with commerce, and with various subsidiary aspects of commercial activity, such as travelling, weighing and measuring, and keeping order in the markets and in the town generally; a familiar example is *aduana* (French, *douane*) meaning a customs-house, from the Arabic *dīwān*. Another sphere with many words is house-building; the words are mostly for parts of the house or its furnishings which indicate a degree of comfort beyond the bare necessities. Irrigation has a number of Arabic words; and there is a plethora of fruits, vegetables and other species of food. Army matters are included, and terms from various industries and crafts. Most curious are a few words like *iarifo*, "showy", which might be regarded as proceeding from a degree of urban sophistication in the assessment of character.[4] An economic historian, not especially of Spain, has summed the matter up by saying that "if the north wanted the best in science, medicine, agriculture, industry or civilised living, it must go to Spain to learn".[5]

Finally, the question must be raised—but not answered—whether there was an inevitable tension between this commerce-based urban civilisation of southern Spain and the mainly agricultural and pastoral civilisation of the north. There was something about the economy of the north and its geographical features that made feudalism the best way of achieving a measure of security, so that it was adopted even by the Muslims. Islamic civilisation had its appropriate material basis in the mixed economy of Mediterranean "dry" farming, industry and commerce. Are we justified in seeing the struggle between Christians and Muslims in Spain as taking up into itself this tension between a political organisation suited to a primitive economy and that suited to a more advanced urban and mercantile economy? Was either cultural system capable of absorbing the other type of economy?

3. *Social and Religious Movements*

Unfortunately there is not nearly as much known as might be wished about social and religious movements in al-Andalus. What will be said here, though following the opinions generally held by contemporary scholars, is based not on any thorough study of the sources but on a comparatively small number of facts which scholars happen to have noticed. With this warning a conspectus may be given of the different elements in the society of the tenth century.

The Berbers may be considered first, since they are relatively easy to deal with. They seem to have come mostly from the sedentary, not the nomadic Berbers. Most of them probably went to swell the rural proletariat, though a few found their way to the cities and engaged there in humble crafts. One or two, however, became noted in the religious sciences. They were all Muslims. Some of their ancestors had doubtless become Muslims in order to share in the Arab conquests and the wealth to be gained thereby. Those who emigrated to al-Andalus after the first wave of conquest may have been attracted chiefly by the higher standard of living there, and perhaps by the slightly greater security. Once settled in al-Andalus there was need for solidarity with the other Muslims, especially the Arabs, in the face of a certain amount of hostility from the non-Muslim population. It is perhaps largely for this reason that the heretical forms of Islam prominent in North Africa did not take root in Spain. Khārijite doctrine in North Africa had become an expression of the anti-Arab feelings of the nomadic Berbers, and was therefore not attractive to the sedentary Berbers now in al-Andalus, who were conscious of their need for Arab support. Shīʿite doctrine, centred in the conception of the charismatic leader or holy man, was perhaps more naturally attractive to them; but in this case also the need for Arab-Berber solidarity would hold them back from following any leader who was likely to divide them from the Arabs. The man who claimed to be the Mahdī in 901 (cf. p. 44) led his followers against non-Muslims and not against Arabs.

The Arabs, though only a small section of the inhabitants of al-Andalus, gave a certain colour to the whole civilisation. Here, however, we come upon one of the central problems in the history of Islamic culture in Spain. How strong was the religious and cultural influence of the Arabs? In what precise forms did it manifest itself? How did it come to be so strong? It is easy to understand in a general way the basis of Arab influence. In the heartlands of Islam the period of the Umayyad caliphate of Damascus is regarded as one of Arab domination. This is in contrast to the ʿAbbāsid period in which Persian elements came to the fore. From the conquest until 750 al-Andalus was a province of the Umayyad caliphate of Damascus, and then for another two and a half centuries it was ruled by the Umayyad family. There was much more to it, however, than the mere fact of rule. The Arabs were characterised by intense self-confidence or belief in themselves; and this, coupled with their superior economic position—they had lands in the richest parts of the country—must have led the other sections of the population to admire and emulate them. At first non-Arabs who became Muslims were clients of members of Arab tribes, and often adopted the patron's genealogy; in course of time the point at which the genealogy became fictitious was forgotten, and the clients began to pass themselves off as pure Arabs.

This "arabising" of Spain appears at many points—the name "Mozarabs" (meaning "arabisers") for the Christian living under Muslim rule, the interest in Arab genealogy and other questions of Arab origins, the dominance of the distinctively Arabian Mālikite legal rite, and above all the popularity of the language. It is not clear that the original Arab invaders and settlers brought much culture with them. What was probably more important was that they remained in contact with the Arabic-speaking lands in the Middle East, and were therefore able to benefit from the cultural advances made there.

Much more numerous than the Arabs in the strict sense were the *muwallads* or Muslims of Iberian stock. In course of time many of them adopted purely Arab genealogies; the writer Ibn-Ḥazm (p. 128) actually claimed descent from an arabised Persian. The confusion brought about by such genealogies was not serious from any practical point of view. Descent was reckoned only in the male line, but the original Arabs had married Iberian women freely, so that by the tenth century there was no clear racial distinction between Arabs and *muwallads*. It is therefore not surprising that the two groups became more and more fused into one.

Little is known in detail about the reasons for the acceptance of the Islamic religion by so many inhabitants of the Iberian peninsula. The existing state of affairs may have had something to do with it.[6] There was a high degree of co-operation—or should we say "collusion"?—between the Visigothic ruling group and the ecclesiastical authorities, which made life very uncomfortable for those who for any reason, material or theological, did not accept all the rulings of the ecclesiastics. Among the latter may be reckoned many slaves and the remaining pagans; but it is also possible that for some the traces of the Arian heresy so long professed by the Goths (according to which Jesus was little more than a man) eased the path to conversion to Islam on the intellectual side. For the Christian nobles and the numerous members of the lower and middle classes of town-dwellers there was doubtless a mixture of material and religious motives. Among these motives a prominent place would be held by desire for the social advantages of being a Muslim and admiration for the culture associated with Islam.

Yet, when allowance has been made for all available facts, there remains a puzzle about the acceptance of Islamic culture by so many of the people of Spain. On the one hand, a century before the conquest of Spain by the Arabs their ancestors had been living a very rough life in the steppes of Arabia, and the actual invaders had had little time to acquire a high level of culture. On the other hand, a tradition of learning had been established at Seville by Isidore (d. 636), which had made that city one of the leading intellectual centres of Christian Europe. Yet this Isidorian tradition was abandoned for that of the Arabs and Arabic literature. How is it to be explained? Did the association of the ecclesiastical scholars with the rulers cut them off from the common people? Or was Isidorian culture always restricted to a small handful of men? Or was there some other factor of which we are not fully aware?

It seems clear that the *muwallads* had nothing distinctively Iberian in which they took pride. The great Hungarian Islamist, Ignaz Goldziher, after studying the Shuʿūbite movement in Iraq and Persia, examined materials about Spain to discover traces of it there. In the east this was a literary movement which attacked the supposed superiority of the Arabs and vaunted instead the glories of the Iranian peoples. All that Goldziher was able to find was a couple of judges of Huesca at the beginning of the tenth century who "passionately upheld the cause of the *muwallads*", and a literary epistle of the middle of the eleventh century which repeated arguments of eastern Shuʿūbite writers.[7] From this the conclusion is that, though the *muwallads* were sometimes annoyed at the Arab assumption of superiority, they had nothing positive of their own to oppose to it.

The next important group, the Mozarabs or Christians living under Muslim rule, shows this same fascination of things Arab. In 854 a Christian writer described the situation thus:

> Our Christian young men, with their elegant airs and fluent speech, are showy in their dress and carriage, and are famed for the learning of the gentiles; intoxicated with Arab eloquence they greedily handle, eagerly devour and zealously discuss the books of the Chaldeans (i.e. Muhammadans), and make them known by praising them with every flourish of rhetoric, knowing nothing of the beauty of the Church's literature, and looking down with contempt on the streams of the Church that flow forth from Paradise; alas! the Christians are so ignorant of their own law, the Latins pay so little attention to their own language, that in the whole Christian flock there is hardly one man in a thousand who can write a letter to inquire after a friend's health intelligibly, while you may find a countless rabble of all kinds of them who can learnedly roll out the grandiloquent periods of the Chaldean tongue. They can even make poems, every line ending with the same letter, which display high flights of beauty and more skill in handling metre than the gentiles themselves possess.[8]

This passage makes it clear to what an extent the Christians of al-Andalus, even while remaining Christians, were carried away by admiration for Arab civilisation. It should, of course, be conceded that this description applies chiefly to town-dwellers, and that a high percentage of Mozarabs may not have been town-dwellers. The fact that the interest is above all in the language and in poetry argues that up to the middle of the ninth century the distinctively Arab elements had been most prominent in al-Andalus, or at least had appealed most to the Iberian population. Despite the acceptance of Arab civilisation, however, the Mozarabs were not wholly satisfied. They supported Muwallad risings, like that of Ibn-Ḥafṣūn; and from the latter part of the ninth century many of them emigrated from al-Andalus to the Christian kingdoms. Like the Muwallads they commonly spoke a romance dialect, though the more educated were able to write in Arabic as well as to speak it.

Other groups in the country were the Jews and the slaves. The Jews stood somewhat apart from the general life of the country, though they came to have a share in its intellectual life. Among the slaves and ex-slaves a distinction was made between the negroes and the "Slavs" (Ṣaqāliba). The latter included not merely persons of Slav race but also Franks and other slaves from the north. While the influx doubtless began earlier, it was especially under ʿAbd-ar-Raḥmān III that large numbers were imported for the army and for the service of the palace. Some, but by no means all, were eunuchs. A few rose to positions of power and influence. Most were eventually freed and usually settled in the towns, so that by the eleventh century they constituted an important element in the population, with a place in politics out of proportion to their numbers. It would appear that they normally became Muslims. Christians also, however, seem to have had slaves, and these would presumably be Christian.

These, then, were the main groups in the population of al-Andalus. The general social and religious trends can be roughly discerned, and one thus gains some idea of the problems of creating and maintaining unity in the Umayyad state.

4. *The Ruling Institution*

The Umayyad state of al-Andalus was first and foremost an autocracy. Everything was, at least theoretically, in the hands of the emir or caliph, though according to his inclinations he might delegate much of the detail of administration or even, as in the case of al-Ḥakam II, much of the general control of policy. In the hands of the head of state was the responsibility for internal and external affairs, and the supreme command of the army. His also was the power of life and death, solely at his will. Various marks of dignity were gradually adopted setting him off from his subjects and making access to him difficult. This was especially the case after the assumption of the caliphate in 929. Up to that date, for example, the preacher at the Friday midday worship (or prayers) had invoked God's blessing on the 'Abbāsid caliph in Baghdad as the rightful head of the community of Muslims, although politically he was not recognised in any way; but from 929 it was the name of 'Abd-ar-Raḥmān III an-Nāṣir which was mentioned instead.

There was usually a chief minister with the title of *ḥājib* or "chamberlain". His office was much the same as that of the vizier (*wazīr*) in the east; but in al-Andalus the vizierate was a minor dignity conferred on several subordinate ministers. These men were in charge of a large central secretariat, housed in the palace of the Umayyads at Cordova, and mostly continuing there when the caliph and his court, about the middle of the tenth century, moved to the new palace-city of Madīnat az-Zahrā', some three miles out of Cordova. There was a small replica of this central administration in each of the twenty-one or more provinces (*kuwar*, sing. *kūra*) into which al-Andalus (apart from the Marches) was divided. Each province was under a governor or *wālī*. The non-Muslims had a certain measure of autonomy. They were organised in groups or communities in the various provinces, and at the head of each group, and responsible for its poll-tax (*jizya*), was a *comes* or count (Ar. *qūmis*). They also had their own judges.[9]

The system of three Marches for the defence of the northern frontier has already been described (p. 34). Little more need be said about the armed forces. Mercenaries were first used by al-Ḥakam I (796–822), and the numbers gradually increased. Many were Franks and Slavs, originally slaves; and latterly there were also Berbers from North Africa and negroes. Certain of the mercenaries constituted the personal guard of the ruler. Apart from the mercenaries a considerable number of citizens were liable to military service, the former *jundīs* (who had been given fiefs in return for military service) and townsmen. A third section was that of the volunteers for the holy war, whom the ruler called for specially when he was about to make an expedition against the Christian kingdoms.

Though the jurists are not part of the administration in the strict sense, they belong in a fashion to the ruling institution. In the east the jurists had acted as the leaders of a sort of "constitutionalist" party within the caliphate, and had insisted that in many spheres government should be in accordance with the Sharī'a or revealed law. In this way they had created a counterweight to the autocratic tendencies of rulers and given ordinary men a measure of security; there remained spheres, however, such as the relations of the caliph to his courtiers, where the principles of the Sharī'a were not applied. In certain respects, too, the jurists had come to be dominated by the ruling institution, since it was responsible for making the appointments to the best positions that were open to jurists. This led to widespread worldliness among the jurists and other scholars.[10]

How far this situation, which was found at the centre of the 'Abbāsid caliphate, was paralleled in al-Andalus is a question which has not been adequately studied. The dominant legal rite in al-Andalus was the Mālikite (as will be seen in the next chapter), and the influence of the jurists seems to have grown steadily. They are said to have had more influence under al-Ḥakam II (961–76) than under his father, 'Abd-ar-Raḥmān III. The general impression given by a rapid survey of events is that the jurists of al-Andalus of the tenth century had less influence than those of Iraq. It likewise seems doubtful whether (as is sometimes asserted) the Umayyads deliberately used the Islamic religion to bring unity and harmony to their heterogeneous realm. Various points have been noted in previous chapters which suggest that up to the later tenth century, at least, the

Arabic element in the culture of the Muslims was more influential than the Islamic.

Nevertheless there are some reasons for thinking that Islamic influence was growing. Al-Andalus remained in touch with the heartlands of the Islamic world, and the next chapter will show what this meant in the intellectual and literary spheres. The Muslims clearly thought of Baghdad as setting the standard by which everything must be measured. Although the claims of the 'Abbāsid caliphs to political suzerainty were rejected, we find items of the court ceremonial of Baghdad being adopted in Cordova in the later tenth century, and perhaps even something of the form of administration practised by the 'Abbāsids. It would be wrong, however, to conclude that this imitation of Baghdad was due to sheer admiration; it might have been much more a concern for efficient administration. The administration of al-Andalus, it must be remembered, developed from the forms of the later Umayyad caliphate of Damascus, where the weaknesses of the old Arab system were being realised and interest was being shown in Persian methods. As time went on and the problems facing the rulers of al-Andalus became more serious, they may well have been impressed by the practical advantages of the Baghdad system; information about it could have been obtained directly from Baghdad or indirectly from Cairouan, which, prior to its conquest by the Fāṭimids in 909, was the capital of a state partly dependent on Baghdad.

There is practically nothing in the organisation of the ruling institution that is derived from the Visigothic tradition. The former close association of the ecclesiastical hierarchy with the rulers may have facilitated the growth of the influence of the jurists in the Islamic state, but it was not the source of this tendency. Apart from this the chief point appears to be, as noted above, the adoption of quasi-feudalistic ideas by the emirs and caliphs in their dealings with the Christian kingdoms in the north.

(5)

CULTURAL ACHIEVEMENTS UNDER THE UMAYYADS

1. *Intellectual Life — The Religious Sciences*

THE focal point of Muslim intellectual activity has always been law or jurisprudence. Yet a statement of this kind tends to be misleading to the average reader, since the Islamic conception of law differs in various ways from every other. The word usually translated "Islamic law" is *sharī'a*, but the basic meaning of this is "what is revealed". So the Sharī'a in the modern sense is not to be compared with any code of positive law. There are a few definite enactments in the Qur'ān, and these are taken up into the Sharī'a, but this was far from sufficing even the needs of the community of Medina during the lifetime of Muḥammad, still less the needs of a great empire. So Muḥammad's practice and the continuation of this practice by his successors in office was taken into consideration also. The curious thing about the whole development is that, besides those who were responsible for the administration of justice, many men became interested in discussing questions of jurisprudence from a rather theoretical point of view. The root of their interest seems to have been the desire to ensure that the Islamic community, as it was founded on a "revealed law", should remain entirely faithful to that law.[1]

This theoretical or religious concern of the jurists (if this term may be applied prematurely to these early thinkers) was pursued by them without any direct reference to the ruling institution. Sometimes men from their ranks might be judges in the service of the institution; sometimes certain jurists might feel very critical of the actions of the institution and consider that it had departed from the "revealed law". This was particularly so under the Umayyad caliphate of Damascus (up to 750); the ʿAbbāsids tended to defer to the opinions of the jurists, at least ostensibly. This bifurcation between the jurists and the actual rulers meant that the conclusions of the jurists were not automatically put into practice, but only in so far as the rulers decided that they were to be the basis of action. The jurists indeed discussed much more than legal matters in the modern sense, for they included what we would call etiquette and liturgical forms. The "revealed law" was a whole "revealed way of life".

At first the discussions were chiefly at the level of the ethical conceptions implicit in the actual practice of the community, and it was assumed that this practice was being continued unchanged. By about the beginning of the second Islamic century (about 720 A.D.), however, it was realised that changes were beginning to creep in, and that in various regions of the Islamic world there were different versions of what Muḥammad's practice had in fact been. From this time the activity of the jurists had two aspects. Firstly, they had to decide whether, in any given circumstances, the act was in accordance with the "revealed law". Secondly, they had to formulate the basic conceptions or "roots" of law in such a way as to justify in self-consistent fashion all their particular decisions. It came to be universally accepted that the "revealed law" was expressed not merely in the Qur'ān but in the regular practice—the "beaten path" or *sunna*—of Muḥammad. It also came to be accepted that Muḥammad's practice was known only through duly authenticated Traditions (in the technical sense, marked here by a capital, of anecdotes about

Muḥammad). Most jurists further held that particular prescriptions could be derived from the Qur'ān and the Traditions by various rational procedures (such as analogical argument), but there was considerable discussion about which procedures were permissible. Yet a fourth "root" was sometimes recognized, the consensus of the community (*ijmā'*).

Between about 800 and 900 the main trends of thought on legal matters hardened into schools or rather rites—the latter word is preferable when referring to differences in practice rather than in theory. Some of these rites, such as the Ẓāhirite which had a notable exponent in Spain, died out after a time. Among the Sunnites, or main body of Muslims, four rites came to be recognised as permissible variants—the Ḥanafite, the Mālikite, the Shāfi'ite and the Ḥanbalite. So far as al-Andalus is concerned the only one of these which is important is the Mālikite, which derives its name from Mālik ibn-Anas (d. 795), who belonged to the school of Medina. It is usually stated that at first the Muslims of Spain followed the teaching of a Syrian jurist, al-Awzā'ī, and later, about 800, went over officially to the school of Mālik. This is roughly true, but some refinements are necessary.

The administration of justice in al-Andalus was formally in the hands of the ruler, whether governor appointed from Damascus, independent emir, or caliph; but he usually delegated responsibility to special persons for this function. At first these were politicians rather than jurists. Even under the emir 'Abd-ar-Raḥmān I there was no class of jurists, though there were a few men who had studied jurisprudence in the heartlands of the Islamic world. One such was Ṣa'ṣa'a (d. 796 or 807), who studied in Syria under al-Awzā'ī (d. 773) and others, presumably before the fall of the Umayyads there in 750. Since al-Awzā'ī was the leading jurist of the province in which the capital lay it was natural that his views should be followed in the distant province of al-Andalus, and should continue to be followed when it became an independent state under members of the Umayyad family.

After 750 al-Awzāʿī, settled in Beirut and outwardly, though perhaps not inwardly, reconciled to the ʿAbbāsid régime, was out of touch with the leading politicians and much less influential than he had been. Students still seem to have come from al-Andalus to hear his lectures, but they also went to Medina and other places.[2] In Medina the views on the principles of jurisprudence propounded by Mālik and several other teachers were similar to those of al-Awzāʿī, but slightly further developed;[3] both were simple and primitive compared with the thinking of the Shāfiʿites and Ḥanafites in Iraq. In this situation, it probably did not much matter whether the jurists of al-Andalus professed to follow al-Awzāʿī or Mālik, since in neither case would their views be regarded as absolutely authoritative by the rulers.

A real change seems to have come about when two young jurists from Cairouan, one of whom had studied in Iraq, systematically arranged a large number of questions on particular points of law, and recorded the answers given to them in Cairo by one of Mālik's pupils. The books of these two jurists, containing the questions and answers, thus constituted a codification of the Sharīʿa on Mālikite principles, and would be very useful for practical purposes. The earlier of the two books was apparently introduced into al-Andalus about 800 by ʿĪsā ibn-Dīnār (d. 827) and Yaḥyā ibn-Yaḥyā al-Laythī (d. 847), the latter being a Berber. The emir al-Ḥakam I (796–822) apparently gave some official recognition to this codification of the Mālikite rite, so that from this time onwards it was the official rite in Spain. It was widely taught, and the Mālikite jurists came to be a cohesive group.[4] There was apparently little further discussion of the general principles of jurisprudence at this period, but there was some intellectual activity concerned with elaborating particular prescriptions and applying

PLATE 5. Detail of Ivory work on a casket fashioned in Cordova.

PLATE 6. Oil lamp in wrought bronze (Alhambra Museum, Granada)

PLATE 7. Ivory casket from the time of the Caliphate at Cordova. Mozarab craftsmanship

them to Spanish conditions. 'Īsā ibn-Dīnār was the author of a work in twelve volumes. The most notable production however, was by a slightly later jurist, al-'Utbī (d. 869), and was apparently supplementary to the early works of codification.

The establishment of a body of Mālikite jurists may thus be regarded as the chief intellectual activity in the sphere of religion in al-Andalus under the Umayyads. The aims of these jurists were practical rather than theoretical, and they worked in close association with the Mālikite jurists of Cairouan and other parts of North Africa. That Spain and North Africa should have attached themselves to the Mālikite rite in preference to all others is not entirely fortuitous. In Iraq where the Ḥanafite and Shāfi'ite rites were developed many of the Muslims belonged to the pre-Islamic population of the region and, before their conversion, had been under the influence of Hellenistic culture. In North Africa and the Iberian peninsula, on the other hand, the Arabs were the bearers of the dominant intellectual culture; the Berbers had had little of their own, and the Iberians, for reasons that are not altogether clear, preferred that of the Arabs to the Latin culture of the Isidorian revival. Because of the essentially Arab outlook of these regions, without any admixture of the speculative interest of Hellenism, it was only natural that the simple and essentially Arab Mālikite rite should have most appeal, and that within Mālikism the eminently practical form worked out in Cairouan should be favoured. It is also possible that in peripheral regions like these—one thinks of the comparison with the form of British culture in, say, Canada or Australia—there was a tendency to cling to orthodoxy; but it is difficult to say what could be meant by "orthodoxy" here, and, whatever meaning is given to it, it would seem that the desire for something simple and practical was more influential.

It is commonly stated that the other legal rites had no

followers in Spain, but this is not quite exact. It may be that they were not officially recognised nor provided for in the courts, but on the other hand Ibn-Ḥazm (d. 1064) appears to have received Shāfiʿite teaching in al-Andalus. The most notable of those who are alleged to have held Shāfiʿite views was Baqī ibn-Makhlad (d. 889). Like most of the leading jurists and scholars of al-Andalus at this time he had studied in the heartlands of the Islamic world, but unlike most of the others he had become interested in the speculative aspects of jurisprudence and the derivation of legal prescriptions from Traditions. On his return, whether because of his general ideas or because he taught Traditions, he incurred the hostility of the Mālikites, but was able to remain active in Cordova through the protection of the emir Muḥammad I (852–86). Certainly the study of Traditions, however frowned upon by the strict Mālikites, began to take root in Spain.

Nearly a century later one of the leading figures in legal circles in al-Andalus had the reputation of being a Ẓāhirite —an adherent of the rite to which the later Ibn-Ḥazm belonged, but which eventually disappeared. This was al-Mundhir ibn-Saʿīd al-Ballūṭī, who was the chief judge or qāḍī of Cordova from 950 until his death in 966 at the age of eighty-two. In the cases of al-Mundhir and Baqī the ideas objected to by the Mālikites must have been regarded as private opinions on secondary matters, and cannot have been propagated widely. The support that they received from the rulers is a point to be noticed, for among other things it suggests that the rulers up to this period were not prepared to allow the Mālikites a monopoly.

There are slight traces in al-Andalus of some of the other intellectual currents found in the heartlands. In the works of biography, for example, it is recorded of one or two men that they held certain doctrines usually associated with the Muʿtazilites, a sect of semi-philosophical theologians prominent in Iraq in the first half of the ninth century.[5] The bellettrist al-Jāḥiẓ (d. 868), who was greatly admired and read in al-Andalus, was a Mu'tazilite, and admiration for him may have contributed to the acceptance of Mu'tazilite ideas. As a whole, however, Mu'tazilism did not take root in al-Andalus. More deeply influenced by Greek philosophy was Ibn-Masarra (d. 931), whose views, though not well known, appear to have contained Empedoclean elements. The opposition to him from the Mālikites of Cordova was such that he retired to a hermitage in the neighbouring Sierra, where he was able to instruct and "form" a small number of disciples, and perhaps to lay the foundations of Andalusian mysticism.[6]

In general, then, it can be said that up to the end of the tenth century the best developed field of study was the Mālikite doctrine of the "branches" or detailed legal prescriptions. Of the other "religious sciences"—it is convenient to use this translation for the Arabic word *'ulūm*, "knowledges", which is also used for the natural sciences —a beginning had been made with the study of Traditions and with the exegesis (*tafsīr*) of the Qur'ān. Some individuals held views on the "roots" of law and on matters of theology (*kalām*), but these can hardly be said to have existed as disciplines. (Grammar and lexicography, which were needed for Qur'ānic exegesis, were studied, but they will be dealt with in the next section.) Of the "foreign sciences" (that is, Greek thought), philosophy was not cultivated apart from that of Ibn-Masarra, but from about 950 there was some advanced study of medicine, while al-Ḥakam II (961–76) encouraged astronomy and mathematics.

Apart from the books on Mālikite law, important works in the field of history and biography were also produced. Islamic historiography had its roots partly in the northern Arabs' interest in genealogy and the heroic achievements of their tribes, and partly in Iranian (and to a lesser extent Christian) historiographical tradition. It may be said to have come of age in the heartlands by about 900. That the culture of al-Andalus was still part of general Islamic culture is shown by the fact that a native of Spain, ʿArīb (d.c. 980), achieved fame as the continuator for the Hijra years 291 to 320 (A.D. 904–32) of the history of aṭ-Ṭabarī, the greatest of early Arabic histories. Apart from this, most of the historical and biographical writing in Spain was at first on matters of local interest. The first person who can claim to be called a historian is Aḥmad ar-Rāzī (d. 953), whose work is the basis of the Spanish document known as the *Crónica del Moro Rasis*. About the same time biographical works, now lost, were compiled about the scholars of Cordova and other towns. There has been preserved, however, a *History of the Judges of Cordova*, written by a scholar from Cairouan who settled there, by name al-Khushanī (d. 971 or 981).[7] These scanty details are sufficient to show how, with the access of wealth and power under ʿAbd-ar-Raḥmān III, the Muslims of al-Andalus became aware of themselves as a distinctive unit within the Islamic community, and thereby grew in self-confidence.

2. *Intellectual Life — Poetry and Belles-Lettres*

When—with the advent of Islam and the conquest of an Empire—the Arabs first strode on to a world stage, they already had fine lines to declaim. Their poets were no fumbling beginners, responding to the stimulus of a new-found greatness, but had a treasury of resonant odes. Each of these followed a fixed form; they usually started with an erotic prelude, then moved through a succession of conventional themes—description of camels or horses, of hunting scenes and battles—to culminate in the praise of some noble chieftain or valiant tribe. Conventions and clichés abounded: at the outset, the poet was assumed to be travelling through the desert with only one or two companions, and to have come across barely discernible traces of an encampment "like tattoo-marks amid the arteries of the wrist", in which he recognised a site on which once dwelt a woman he had loved. The odes also had elaborate metres, and a single rhyme throughout. Everything in them bespoke a well-established tradition, a tradition which has seldom been challenged until modern times.

True, the life of the conquering Muslims was no longer that of the desert nomads. Indeed, as the Arabs were derided by their more sophisticated subjects as "camel-drivers and lizard-eaters", they were not slow to adopt Persian manners or to study Greek thought; but they were —as is natural—slower to absorb aesthetic values and they showed very little interest in Greek literature, steeped as it was in pagan legend. On the contrary, in the battle of words that raged between Arabs and non-Arabs in the early Muslim empire, the twin glories of which the Arabs could boast without fear of being gainsaid by detractors who had accepted Islam were the revelation specially vouchsafed to their race, and the language in which this revelation was couched and which was essential to its understanding. With this language, pre-Islamic poetry was indisssolubly linked. The conservatism inherent in the pre-Islamic tradition, born of the unchanging life of the desert, was reinforced as it became a bastion of racial pride.

Changes in literary practice did occur, as was inevitable. Subsidiary themes of the ode were developed into independent love-songs and wine-songs. The descriptive powers of the desert poet who recorded with a strangely impersonal, photographic eye alike the beauty spot on a young woman's face and the droppings of a gazelle upon the sands were enriched by an emotional response to a more bountiful nature, and extended to castles and ships and other man-made wonders. Indeed the latter part of the eighth century—coinciding with the establishment of the Umayyad emirate in Spain—was in the East a period of bold innovation when Abū-Nuwās (d. 803) openly ridiculed and parodied the traditional ode and Abū-'l-'Atāhiya (d. 826) brought the language of the market place into court. Yet when all this effervescence had subsided, what remained to slake the thirst of countless generations of Arabic-speaking intellectuals was the traditional beverage with but one strong new flavour added: rhetorical artifice. The supremacy of the Ancients was admitted, and the ideal formation of a poet was taken to be acquaintance with and emulation of their odes. The structure and metres of poems were traditional. Even the themes were mostly limited to conventional ones. What was expected of the living poet was increasing refinement of expression within the conventional framework. Some—like al-Mutanabbī (d. 965) in the East—were possessed of such genius that it could burst through these conventions without flouting them, while their critics somewhat lamely tried to explain their greatness in terms of mastery of these very conventions. For most poets, however, the task was one of refurbishing old motifs with increasingly subtle variations, overlaying them with *recherché* similes and daring hyperboles, and the like. In the words of A. J. Arberry:

> Precisely as Saracenic art and architecture, denied the inspiration of the human body, tended inevitably towards the elaboration of arabesque ornament, the infinite subtle variation of geometrical design; so in Arabic poetry the business of the creative craftsman was to invent patterns of thought and sound within the framework of his revered tradition. Poetry became an arabesque of words and meanings.[8]

Evidently this was a poetry for connoisseurs. The common people, even as they evolved regional dialects different from the classical language, no doubt regaled themselves with folk-songs and folk-tales of which we have samples in the *Arabian Nights*; but these the intellectuals scarcely dignified with the name of literature. That which alone was deemed worthy of studying and recording was a poetry which had its outlet principally at the courts of princes, princelings and other imitators. A poet's fortunes depended on securing the favour of a wealthy and powerful patron who would either reward him for a particular panegyric or attach him to his service. If he possessed other qualities as well, his poetic attainments could open for him the door to high office; but in itself his position was a subservient one. He addressed himself primarily not to the inarticulate masses who needed to have their experience expressed, extended or refined, but to a cultured élite well versed in the rules of his craft and prepared to delight in, or pass judgement on, his virtuosity.

Thus conditioned by the standards of an élite that valued literary tradition and refinement of expression above all else, Arabic poetry is remarkable for its continuity from generation to generation, and its homogeneity even under different climes. It is in incidental details and subtle overtones that reflections of local conditions and cultural changes are to be sought.

Essentially, the Arabic poetry produced in al-Andalus was an offshoot of that produced in the East; and in the period now under review, it was little more than that. ʿAbd-ar-Raḥmān I had a country-seat identical with his uncle's near Damascus, like it called ar-Ruṣāfa, and to him are ascribed a few lines of poetry which begin:

Emerging before us in the midst of ar-Ruṣāfa is a palm-tree
Far, in this Western land, from the home of palm-trees;
I said: Like me is it in my expatriation and my yearning
And in the length of my absence from my children and my kin . . .

Indifferent as the lines are in quality, they show clearly enough where the spiritual home of Spain's earliest poets lay.

For 'Abd-ar-Raḥmān and other newcomers to al-Andalus already had an intellectual formation of which they had cause to be proud, and the Visigoths whom they displaced had no culture so obvious in value as to call for immediate integration into the conquerors'. Indeed a ninth-century Christian writer had cause to complain that fellow-Christians were so taken with the Arabic language and its literature as to neglect, and even express contempt for, Latin texts.[9] For those born and bred to Arabic there was not even a need to choose, and the massive fact about Umayyad Spain is that for all the political rivalry that existed between it and the East, it was to the East that it looked for cultural guidance.

Not only had Andalusian literature grown out of a cutting from the East: it was constantly reinforced and modified by grafts from the East. From Baghdad came the singer Ziryāb (d. 857), disciple and then rival of Is'ḥāq al-Mawṣilī, with his trained children and slave-girls, to found the Andalusian school of music and song and incidentally to teach the manners of Baghdad society. From Baghdad also came the noted scholar Abū-'Alī al-Qālī (d. 965), to be received with great honour and to dictate his voluminous *Amālī*. These were disconnected discourses of primarily lexicographical or grammatical interest, but studded, as is the Arab tradition, with poetic quotations often conveying, if only by implication, literary preferences; they were to have incalculable influence on succeeding generations of Andalusian intellectuals. With surprisingly little lag in time, the compositions of the greatest poets of the East were being studied and imitated in al-Andalus. Indeed, although the older poetry was studied, it was the new taste for rhetorical embellishments that was most strongly reflected in the production of Andalusian poets.

Not surprisingly, al-Andalus did not immediately produce poets of great distinction. There are not a few poets of the late eighth century and of the ninth whose names are recorded and samples of whose compositions have been preserved; but they are no more than competent. Indeed many of them were princes of the Umayyad house who owed to their rank and station the attention they have received from literary historians and anthologists. It was not until late in the Umayyad period—when Cordova had become a centre of learning and the court offered worthy patronage to men of talent and of learning—that al-Andalus produced two men of letters of lasting reputation.

Ibn-ʿAbd-Rabbih (860–940), a poet whose amatory verses are not without charm, is famous above all for his literary thesaurus *Al-ʿIqd al-Farīd* ("The Peerless Necklace"), which proved immensely popular for many centuries both in the East and in the West. He took for his model the work compiled in the East by Ibn-Qutayba (d. 889) and entitled *The Fountains of Story*, and drew his material mostly from the East; in fact, he quoted no Andalusian compositions other than his own. Ibn-ʿAbd-Rabbih was also the author of a 450-line *urjūẓa*—a type of metrical composition less demanding than the classical ode, the hemistiches usually being treated as independent lines and rhymed in couplets—on the warlike exploits of ʿAbd-ar-Raḥmān III; it deserves mention because narrative poems are rare in Arabic in any age.

Undoubtedly the most accomplished Andalusian poet of his time was Ibn-Hāni' (d. 973), but accusations of heresy forced him to leave Spain when he was about twenty-seven years of age and to seek his fortune with the Fāṭimids. He was styled "the Mutanabbī of the West", but this should be taken as an indication of his standing among Andalusians and of his grandiloquence and sententiousness rather than of his genius. Illustrative of his style is this description of the warships of the Fāṭimid ruler al-Muʿizz:

. . . They are proud mountains, except that they move;
Some of them are lofty peaks and some forbidding [heights].
They are birds—but birds of prey
  That have no quarry other than [human] souls.
They are [flints] struck to start an all-consuming fire
  Which when battle is joined proves unextinguishable.
When they breathe hard in anger they fling out a blaze
  Like that with which the fire of Hell is lit.
So their hot mouths are thunderbolts
  And the breath they exhale is iron.

They hold firebrands over the deeps
  Like blood being caught in black sheets.
They embrace the waves of the sea as though it were
  Oil in which they dip trimmed wicks.
The water there, though dark in the main,
  Is like a skin touched [and stained] by the saffron of a
    perfume.
They know no reins other than the winds,
  And no rough terrain other than the foam . . .

This profusion of unassorted images, like debris tumbling down a mountainside, is characteristic of the style that by then prevailed throughout the Arabic-speaking lands. Two features of it will seem strange to Western taste. The first is its fragmentation: the poet does not attempt to build up one consistent image, or induce one consistent mood; this is a phenomenon observable in Arabic poetry from its earliest stages, each idea or conceit being rounded off in one self-sufficient line. The other is the use of imagery in ways which sometimes seem strangely lifeless and aesthetically indifferent, as when awesome fire-carrying ships are compared to night-lights.

Louis Massignon has made the arresting observation that the artistic spirit of Islam tends to "de-realise", to petrify objects so that the metaphor follows a descending gradation: man is compared to animal, animal to flower, flower to precious stone. As regards the past, the poet does not try to relive emotion. He takes the memory as memory, he works with dreams, shades, ghosts. For the idea in Muslim art is not to idolise images, but to go beyond, to the One who makes them move as in a magic lantern or a shadow play, towards the only One who endures.[10] Attractive as this analysis is, it is by no means always true that in the Arabic metaphor the progression is from animate to inanimate. Rather, it seems that the poet is indifferent to the way in which the progression is made. He is content with a juxtaposition of shapes or colours provided only that they coincide in some one respect—the reflection of yellow fire in water and the stain of saffron on human skin—without concern for the very different experiences with which either image may be associated.

Both these features point to an atomism, a concern with independent detail, deeply ingrained in the cultural tradition of the Arabs if not in their make-up, and contrasting sharply with the concern with unity displayed by European men of letters since the days of ancient Greece.

In this important respect, there was as yet no noticeable difference between the poets of al-Andalus and those of the East. Soon, al-Andalus would emerge as the fulcrum of Muslim intellectual life west of Egypt. Relations with Christian courts in the North of Spain and with Byzantium, toleration of Jewish scholars who were to act as translators and intermediaries, access to Greek and even to some Latin sources—these were to enable al-Andalus to form its own cultural blend. It would even seem that intermarriage with Iberians and daily contacts with a population that remained largely Christian and Romance-speaking were colouring the mentality of the Arabs, who were numerically far from dominant in the population. But this was not as yet apparent in the literary production. A few books, now lost, appear to have been written about Andalusian men of letters, and these may be an indication of nascent "national" pride. But the one significant new departure is the appearance of a new form of poetic composition, the *muwashshaḥ* (to be discussed in Chapter 9), said to have been invented by either Muqaddam ibn-Muʿāfā or Muḥammad ibn-Maḥmūd both of whom lived in Cabra, near Cordova, at the beginning of the tenth century.

As for fine prose or *belles-lettres*, the one form that was practised was the epistle, and the scope for this mostly in official correspondence. Secretaries appear to have been numerous in al-Andalus, and their prestige considerable, for we know of three books written about them; but none of these books is extant. It is likely that here again the Andalusians followed the lead of the East: a preference for pithiness in official correspondence, and a growing taste for rhyme and other verbal embellishment.

3. *Art*

Though the study of art lies somewhat apart from the usual fields of the historian, it is important, in dealing with Islamic Spain, to take into consideration the conclusions of the experts in these matters, since the development of Islamic or Moorish art is complementary to the literary and intellectual history of al-Andalus.[11]

The period up to 976 was the creative or formative period of Moorish art during which there appeared the distinctive features and characteristic spirit which are its glory. The outstanding production was the Great Mosque of Cordova, begun by ʿAbd-ar-Raḥmān I and successively enlarged by ʿAbd-ar-Raḥmān II, al-Ḥakam II and (shortly after 976) by al-Manṣūr. A section in the middle was pulled down after the Reconquista to make way for a Christian cathedral, but a vast area remains much as it was at the end of the tenth century.

The oldest part of the mosque marks the unexpected emergence of a new architectural tradition. No exact prototype has been discovered, though there are reminiscences of Umayyad and Syrian buildings. The horse-shoe arch which is used throughout is now known to have been taken over from Visigothic architecture; but the doubling of the arches to give extra height—possibly suggested by Roman aqueducts—is something new. The peak of artistic achievement is usually held to have been in the part added by al-Ḥakam II with its more ornate arches and elaborate decoration, especially round the *miḥrāb* or niche indicating the direction of Mecca.

The other notable artistic achievement was the palace-city of Madīnat az-Zahrā'. Though it was ruined and rendered uninhabitable in 1013, it has recently been in part excavated (and a small section restored), so that it is now possible to have some idea of what it was like during the brief period when it was in use. It was not strictly utilitarian, though it was well used, but was rather an expression of the self-confidence of the first caliph. No effort was spared to make it a thing of matchless beauty. The lay-out of the walls is in the Roman and Byzantine tradition, and so is the decoration. Byzantine sculptors may even have been brought to Cordova for the purpose. Al-Ḥakam II is likewise said to have brought Byzantine workers in mosaics.

Besides these great architectural works and a number of fortified castles belonging to the same period, there were also small articles in various media from ivory and marble to inlaid gold work and crystal (the latter having been discovered at Cordova about 850). A good tradition in metal work was inherited from Visigothic Spain, but the other crafts were mainly developed under the Muslims, sometimes on the basis of oriental techniques.

Moorish art seems a fusion of oriental and occidental, although it is difficult to pin-point the separate elements. As was only natural most of the materials and techniques used were those of Visigothic Spain. The decorative motifs show considerable Hellenistic influence, some of which certainly came through Visigothic Spain, though some possibly came from the hellenised art of Syria. For long, indeed, the art of Islamic Spain showed traces of the Umayyad art of Syria, with all the influences which it had absorbed. As late as the time of ʿAbd-ar-Raḥmān III the new minaret of the Mosque of Cordova was square in cross-section like the minarets of Syria which had been modelled on church towers. It is in the additions to the Mosque by his successor al-Ḥakam II that Baghdadian influences become clearly marked; and this was the period, of course, when definite efforts were being made to assimilate the intellectual culture of the heartlands.

How is this fusion of cultures to be described? At one point Henri Terrasse speaks of an expression "in an Islamic dress of the soul of Spain"; but a few lines lower he says that "Umayyad Spain attained, for all its temporary political cohesion, an ever more affirmed unity of thought and life",[12] and this would imply that the civilisation was primarily Arab and Muslim. Is it then in essence something Spanish or Arab or Muslim? The energy to expand into Spain and there create the Umayyad state came from the drive of Arab peoples guided by the conceptions of Islamic religion. Yet into this community were incorporated not only Berbers but also many of the Iberian population; and the incorporation was a genuine integration into a "unity of thought and life". Each of the two formulations seems to express an aspect of the truth.

4. *The Source of Moorish Culture*

The reflections on Moorish art of the previous pages require to be complemented by a consideration of similar questions in the literary and intellectual sphere. Here the distinction between Arab and Islamic elements comes to the fore.

As has been noticed at various points above there is much to suggest that at first the Arab element was dominant. This was only natural in a state which had originally been a province of the caliphate of Damascus, characterised above all by Arabism. The chief aesthetic form among the Arabs was language and poetry, and somehow or other the fascination for the Arabs of their own language communicated itself to many of the other inhabitants of the peninsula, including the Mozarabs. As a result of this it was natural that there should be a strong interest in poetry and philology. The acceptance of the Mālikite legal rite, too, was in keeping with the practical and non-speculative Arab outlook.

Yet there was also a will to belong to the great community of Muslims, and to keep in touch with the distinctively Islamic developments of thought in the heartlands. Throughout the Umayyad emirate and caliphate nearly all the leading jurists made the "journey" to the East to sit at the feet of the great teachers there. It has been noted how, as early as 822, the aesthete Ziryāb was given a warm welcome at the court of Cordova, and became an arbiter of fashion in many fields until his death in 857.

The most important steps, however, towards maintaining continuity with the literary and intellectual outlook of Baghdad were taken in the tenth century, first of all by 'Abd-ar-Raḥmān III but chiefly by al-Ḥakam II. Poetry and belles-lettres had attracted attention before this, and the anthology of Abū-Tammām (d. 846) and a work on rhetoric by al-Jāḥiẓ (d. 869) had been brought to Spain in the reign of Muḥammad I (852–86) by returning scholars,[13] while the works of Ibn-Qutayba (d. 889) were known by 910.[14] It was 'Abd-ar-Raḥmān III, however, who welcomed the great philologist al-Qālī in 941. It must have been about this time, too, and so probably with some encouragement from the court, that 'Arīb was making his summary and continuation of the history of aṭ-Ṭabarī. Advantage was also taken of the Fāṭimid occupation of Cairouan to encourage Sunnite scholars, uneasy in the new conditions, to settle in al-Andalus.

Al-Ḥakam II had himself a deep interest in scholarship and bibliography, and set about making the caliphal library one of the largest and best in the Islamic world. It is said eventually to have had over four hundred thousand volumes. He employed the historian ʿArīb as a secretary, though whether for the library is not known. In 963, just after the beginning of the reign, there settled in Cordova a scholar from the east who was an expert in the text of the Qur'ān[15]—a subject which had recently been of political importance in Iraq. This man had some knowledge of Shāfiʿite jurisprudence, but was presumably unable to make use of it because of Mālikite opposition. The arrival in al-Andalus of another eastern expert in the same subject just before the death of the first shows how it was possible to establish in al-Andalus a living tradition of scholarship in the various branches of the "religious sciences".

The above remarks would seem to contradict the view that the distinctively Islamic aspects of the culture of the Muslims were prominent early in the emirate. On the contrary it becomes more and more clear that to begin with the main cultural influence was what has already been called Arabism. Only about the middle of the tenth century through the exuberance following on the successes of the first caliph did the men of al-Andalus contrive to make the Islamic sciences take firm root among them. The suggestion of Lévi-Provençal[16] that ʿAbd-ar-Raḥmān III cultivated Byzantine artistic forms in order to reduce his dependence on Baghdad is surely mistaken, for this is the very period when al-Andalus was making the greatest efforts to establish in itself the Sunnite intellectual traditions of the east.

PLATE 8. Torre del Oro, built by Almohads at beginning of 13th century, at the entrance of Seville on the River Guadalquivir.

(6)

THE COLLAPSE OF ARAB RULE

1. *The ʿĀmirid Dictatorship and the Breakdown*

Caliphs : Hishām II : 976–1013
other six Umayyads : 1009–1031
three Ḥammūdids : 1016–1027
Chamberlains : al-Manṣūr (ibn-Abī-ʿĀmir) : 978–1002
al-Muẓaffar (ʿAbd-al-Malik) : 1002–1008
al-Ma'mūn (ʿAbd-ar-Raḥmān) : 1008–1009

WHEN al-Ḥakam II died in 976 he was succeeded by his son Hishām II, then eleven years old. There were some influential men who wanted a younger brother of al-Ḥakam, since they realised that a regency would be disadvantageous to themselves; but Jaʿfar al-Muṣ'ḥafī, the minister to whom the caliph had entrusted the management of affairs during his illness, acted energetically, and secured both the boy's succession and the continuation of his own power.

In these events al-Muṣ'ḥafī was supported by a man of thirty-eight, often known as Ibn-Abī-ʿĀmir, who came from an old Arab family with lands near Algeciras. Ibn-Abī-ʿĀmir had come to Cordova to study jurisprudence

---

PLATE 9. The Giralda, Seville, once the minaret of the Almohad Mosque, now Cathedral Tower.

and literature, and had been appointed steward to the princess Ṣubḥ to look after the properties and revenues of her son Hishām, whom al-Ḥakam had regarded as his successor. From this fairly humble position Ibn-Abī-ʿĀmir was able to scheme and intrigue his way up the ladder of the civil service until in 976 his influence was an important factor in securing the succession of Hishām. His ambitions were not yet satisfied, however. With uncanny insight into the movement of events and a deep understanding of men's reactions to them, he schemed and calculated—at times in an utterly cold-blooded fashion—until in 978, with support from the general Ghālib, whose daughter he married, he ousted al-Muṣ'ḥafī and himself became *ḥājib* or chamberlain.

In the three following years he was busy strengthening his own position further. One side of his policy was to gain the support of the jurists. A plot against the caliph gave him the opportunity to order the execution of a "Muʿtazilite" opponent of the jurists who was implicated in it. To gain further support he himself copied out the Qur'ān with his own hand, and had many heretical works removed from the library of al-Ḥakam II and burned. Another side of his policy was to reduce the young caliph to impotence. He was encouraged in sensual indulgences and was kept away from contacts and activities which might have prepared him for assuming personal control of state affairs. The princess Ṣubḥ, seeing what was happening to her son, was filled with bitter hatred for her former protégé, said to have been also her lover; but her efforts to alter the situation were easily countered by the astute political climber. The final blow was in 981 when he moved the administration from the caliphal palaces of the Alcazar in Cordova and Madīnat az-Zahrā' to a new palace built by himself and called Al-Madīna az-Zāhira. The caliph was virtually cut off from outside contacts; and it was given out that he had decided to devote himself to piety and to hand over the entire supervision of the affairs of the realm to Ibn-Abī-ʿĀmir.

In this same year of 981 a quarrel developed between Ibn-Abī-ʿĀmir and his father-in-law Ghālib. The latter had some help from the Christian princes of the north, but Ibn-Abī-ʿĀmir with keen foresight summoned from Africa another general with his Berber troops, and placed his reliance on these and on Christian mercenaries. The *jundīs* or men of the levies were grouped in artificial regiments instead of in tribes as previously, and this meant that they were much weaker than they had been. Despite his Christian help Ghālib was defeated and killed. Ibn-Abī-ʿĀmir on his return in triumph to Cordova took the title of al-Manṣūr bi-'llāh ("the one rendered victorious by God"), usually shortened to al-Manṣūr or in the Romance dialects Almanzor. He also was given or took the privilege of having his name mentioned after that of the caliph at the Friday midday worship—a sign that he was of nearly equal rank. As time went on, he received other marks of sovereignty, but he was wise enough not to make any claim of any kind to the caliphal dignity itself. The period from 981 to the death of al-Manṣūr's son al-Muẓaffar in 1008 is thus justifiably referred to as the ʿĀmirid dictatorship, but apart from the fact that al-Manṣūr was both strong and efficient his rule was no more autocratic than that of most other Muslim régimes of the time.

Al-Manṣūr's "reign" is known to have been one of great military activity, but the records are scanty. He is said to have led fifty-seven victorious expeditions. The result of all this activity was an extension of the region definitely held and occupied by Muslims, and the maintenance of a degree of suzerainty over the Christian kingdoms. Christian rulers attempting to break agreements with al-Manṣūr met with severe reprisals. Most of the expeditions were against Leon and Castile or against semi-independent feudal lords within this general area. In 985, however, the

Muslims marched against Barcelona, while 997 saw the great expedition which pillaged and destroyed the church and shrine of Saint James at Compostella in the north-west corner of the peninsula. Only the actual tomb of the saint was left intact. Was it superstition that led al-Manṣūr to make this exception? It certainly enabled the Christians to claim a little later that the saint had been too strong for the Muslims.[1] In the year 1000, however, when several Christian rulers were driven by the disaster to join together to resist the Muslims, the result was one more severe defeat for them. In the closing years of al-Manṣūr Muslim military power was thus supreme practically to the Pyrenees. Indeed, such was the vitality and vigour of al-Andalus that during the same years it was extending its influence in North Africa, so that in 998 al-Manṣūr's son, the future al-Muẓaffar, was able to establish himself in Fez as a kind of viceroy.

When al-Manṣūr died in 1002, apparently worn out by the anxieties of his strenuous career, his son ʿAbd-al-Malik had little difficulty in succeeding to his father's position by obtaining from the caliph Hishām II a grant of similar powers. During his "reign" of six years the position of the Muslims with regard to the Christian kingdoms in the north was more or less maintained, though with increasing difficulty. Constant military activity was required. After a successful expedition in 1007 the caliph decreed for ʿAbd-al-Malik the honorific title of al-Muẓaffar, "the victor", but less than a year later the ruler of al-Andalus was dead in somewhat mysterious circumstances. He had proved, even if not the equal of his father, a competent administrator and a first-class general.

The years from 1008 to 1031 are in some ways one of the most tragic quarter-centuries in all history. From the pinnacle of its wealth, power and cultural achievements al-Andalus fell into the abyss of a bloody civil war. No central authority remained which was able to maintain order throughout the country. Everywhere was confusion. One leader after another appeared, each with his supporting group, and tried to establish effective government at the centre; but one after another had to admit failure. Some lasted only a month or two, none more than two or three years. The nominal (and often also actual) leaders of the various attempts to re-establish central control claimed the dignity of caliph. Besides Hishām II, who was forced to abdicate in 1009 but restored in 1010, six members of the Umayyad family held the caliphate in this period, as well as three members of a half-Berber family known as the Ḥammūdids. The farce was ended in 1031 when a council of ministers meeting in Cordova decreed the abolition of the caliphate and the setting up of a council of state. This council, of course, ruled only the region of Cordova.

The sorry sequence of events was started off by the younger brother who succeeded al-Muẓaffar. He quickly antagonised the people of Cordova, not least by persuading the caliph to declare him heir to the caliphate; and while he was absent in the north they deposed the caliph and set up another Umayyad in his place. Even now the young 'Āmirid did not understand how to retain the loyalty of his army, and he soon perished. Before long, however, the new caliph had lost most of his original support, and it was the turn of a group of Berber officers to gain power for an Umayyad nominee to the caliphate. Next there came to the fore a group of Ṣaqāliba or Slavs, mostly civil servants or mercenary soldiers, likewise with a candidate. So it went on. It is impossible here to give all the details, but it may be noted that the three chief caliph-making groups were the populace of Cordova, the Berbers and the Ṣaqāliba.

By 1031 the thirty towns of any size had a more or less independent ruler. This was the state of affairs which caused the period from 1031 (or from 1009) to be known as the era of the "party kings" or *reyes de taifas* (Ar. *mulūk aṭ-ṭawā'if*).

2. *The Reasons for the Breakdown*

Although the breakdown of the caliphate has a central place in the history of Islamic Spain, the reasons for that breakdown have not been thoroughly investigated. What is to be said here is therefore once again of a provisional character.

The immediately obvious fact underlying the breakdown was what is called "particularism", and this was both local and racial. Difficulties of communication, due to the various mountain ranges probably encouraged the tendency for each region to become an independent political unit. Effective power was in the hands of the local ruler, and only a vast expenditure of energy by the central government could keep the local rulers in check. Also, from about the middle of the tenth century the mixture of races was becoming more of a problem. It is possible that up till then the foreign elements which entered in the eighth century had been largely assimilated. Even where there was little physical intermingling, there seems to have been a degree of cultural homogeneity. In the tenth century however, it became usual to import many slaves from the north and east of Europe, known as Ṣaqāliba or "Slavs", to serve as soldiers and to fill posts in the civil service. Their chief came to have considerable influence. In addition, al-Manṣūr in his rise to power had brought over from Africa fresh contingents of Berbers, whose attitudes were different from those of the long-established Berbers. All these facts indicated that there had been an accentuation of racial divisions.

Though this state of affairs is tolerably clear, it is not clear why it should have become so much more difficult in the early eleventh century to maintain unity. Even if some of those who attempted to re-establish the central government were incompetent, surely they were not all incompetent. Or, if they were, had some change come over the character of the people? We know that wealth had greatly increased under ʿAbd-ar-Raḥmān III, and it may be that the bulk of the population had become so materialistic in outlook that few were capable of the sacrifices needed for unity. This materialistic outlook of the leaders or of their supporters, or both, was very probably one of the factors which lead to the breakdown.

Another line of thought is suggested by keeping in mind the similarities of the situation in Baghdad. There the power had for some time been slipping from the caliph, and in 945 it finally passed into the hands of a family of military leaders; but neither they nor their successors managed to keep control of the full extent of the caliphate. Though the breakdown was never so complete as in al-Andalus and was followed by a partial revival, there is something comparable both to the ʿĀmirid "dictatorship" and to the loss of unity. Could it be, then, that there was either some fundamental defect in Islamic civilisation, or in the whole medieval structure of society? Two points seem to be specially relevant: the failure to adapt Islamic ideas to contemporary problems, and the absence of a strongly-based middle class interested in maintaining an effective central government.

With respect to the first of these points it may be noted that Islam, though it has the name of being a political religion, has not been conspicuously successful in its political ideas.[2] Things went well enough during Muḥammad's lifetime because he was able to adapt existing ideas and institutions to the needs of his growing community. He and his immediate followers, however, were virtually restricted to the political conceptions associated with the Arabian tribe. In one or two matters these proved capable of useful development, namely, in regarding the community of Muslims as comparable to a tribe and communities of non-Muslims as subordinate tribes. Yet such ideas alone were not sufficient in a great empire, and inevitably Persian ideas of statecraft were borrowed, tentatively under the Umayyads of Damascus, and without reserve under the ʿAbbāsids.

Some of these Persian ideas also permeated to Spain. What was noteworthy in Spain, however, as has been already mentioned, was the acceptance of some of the feudal conceptions of Western Europe. Did the Muslim rulers who were prepared to have Christian princes under their suzerainty (while leaving them local autonomy) think they were acting according to Muḥammad's model for the treatment of subordinate communities and fail to notice the differences? Or were they aware of the differences but happily decided to accept local practices? If the latter alternative is near the truth, is it possible that the Islamic religion was less effective than the Christian in giving support to the relationship of a man to his liege-lord (even if the Christian was far from perfect)? Because the political ideas according to which Muslims acted were not closely linked with the basic ideas of Islam as a religion, political activity had little religious sanction and men tended, therefore, to follow self-interest or *raison d'état.* In other words, the chief concern of any régime came to be its own maintenance and not the welfare of those ruled.

The considerations about ideas of a feudal type are most relevant to a discussion of why the Muslims failed to expand in the Iberian peninsula or even to hold what they possessed. Yet they also affect other aspects of the problem, such as military policy. The reason for having fresh Berber and Slav immigrants was to make it possible to keep the Christian princes in check and to expand in North Africa. But were these genuinely Islamic policies, conducive to maintaining a body politic in which men could freely worship God and prepare themselves for facing the Last

Judgement? The rulers of al-Andalus certainly spoke about the holy war; but was this any more than a way of raising the spirits of their troops? The relationship of politics to religion is never an easy matter. Politics has a proper autonomy, and political activities must be guided by political considerations. At times, however, in the Islamic world politics was carried on wholly within a framework of religious ideas; and this was so at some of the more successful periods. Yet elsewhere, as in al-Andalus, politics burst out of the religious framework, and one wonders how much this had to do with the political failure.

The second point for discussion was the absence of a middle class interested in maintaining a strong central government, and some of the matters just mentioned are again relevant. The question of class structure in the medieval orient is not easy. Roughly speaking, it seems to have been the case that there were two classes, an upper class and a lower class. The latter consisted of the urban and rural proletariats; the former, of the rulers, the civil servants and other administrators, the land-owners (often also administrators) and perhaps the great merchants. The intellectuals, of whom the Sunnite jurists are the chief representatives, stood apart, but had come to be largely dependent on the rulers and subservient to them. In so far as the intellectuals performed their function of safeguarding the intellectual basis of Islam they had some influence over the urban proletariat. Otherwise only the upper class was politically active and influential.

It would appear, however, that the effect on the upper class of the increasing wealth of the country (whether al-Andalus or Iraq) was to accentuate the division into groups or cliques, each trying to better itself materially at the expense of the other groups. Seldom in Islamic history had the upper class found its primary motivation in the ideas of religion; and non-religious motivations were certainly strong in al-Andalus at the end of the tenth century. While those in power were ready to *use* religious ideas like the holy war to spur the proletariat to greater efforts, other members of the upper class probably recognised this exploitation for what it was. The expansionist military policy of the 'Āmirids was doubtless regarded by rival cliques as aimed at increasing their own power and glory, rather than simply at keeping the Christian princes in check. In such circumstances there would be little support for the policy among the upper class, and something of this attitude might filter down through the society. The increase of luxury would in any case make many men unwilling to expose themselves to the discomforts and dangers of military campaigns.

At the root of some of the difficulties inherent in this condition of affairs was the failure to develop a religiously-based conception of the function of the upper class in the community of Muslims. There was some idea of the special place of the imām or leader, but there was really nothing between him and the ordinary Muslim. The consequence in practice was that relations between the caliph and the upper class were not guideb dy any religious ideas but by sheer self-interest. There was nothing to foster in any members of the upper class a loyalty to the central government as a structural principle of the community. If they opposed those in power, it could only be from self-interest in the hope of increasing their own share of power. The wealthier members of the proletariat were likewise without any grounds for exerting themselves to preserve the structure of society. The masses could indeed be stirred to vigorous action by religious ideas such as opposition to heretical innovation, but such ideas were largely irrelevant to contemporary circumstances and their application to such circumstances merely opportunist.

Also, it was perhaps the case in al-Andalus that, hidden under its Sunnite exterior, there was an almost Shī'ite respect for the person of the rightful imām. This would be in keeping with the outlook of the peoples of North Africa. That this factor was important is suggested by the reports of the dismay of many when the younger son of al-Manṣūr (who of course had none of the blood of the Prophet's family) got himself declared heir to the caliphate.

These then are some of the factors in the situation of al-Andalus just before the breakdown of the caliphate and of the central government. Before a final evaluation of them can be given much further research is needed.

3. *The "Party Kings"* (1009–91)

Though a semblance of the caliphate continued until 1031, the break-up of the unity of al-Andalus began in 1009. As soon as the central government lost control local governors or other leaders were virtually compelled to take authority into their own hands. On the frontier areas or Marches the disintegration was not so great, since much power was already concentrated in the hands of the commanders there. Thus political units of moderate size continued to exist with their capitals at Badajoz, Toledo and Saragossa in the Lower, Middle and Upper Marches respectively. In the rest of the country the situation was rather different, and in the earlier part of the eleventh century nearly thirty separate political units can be found in or near the south and east coasts. Some did not maintain for long any degree of independence. There were constant intrigues both between the small states and within each, and also constant fighting. A ruler often could not trust his chief minister, and yet had to rely on him; and the members of a ruler's family were frequently plotting to bring about his downfall and replace him.[3] The political history of the period is thus a confused and tangled mass of petty events.

The "parties" (*taifas*, *ṭawā'if*) from whom the "party kings" take the name are the three ethnic groups of Berbers, Ṣaqāliba ("Slavs") and "Andalusians"; the latter included all Muslims of Arab and Iberian stock (and perhaps some descendants of early Berber settlers), who were now almost fused into one so that the Arabs were not reckoned as a separate "party". In any region one "party" tended to be dominant and to rule primarily in its own interests without much thought for the welfare of the rest of the population. Thus there was a lack of unity even in the small states into which Spain was now divided.

The Berbers controlled the south coast from the Guadalquivir to Granada with its seaboard. One notable dynasty was the Ḥammūdid which before 1031 produced three claimants to the caliphate and which ruled Malaga and Algeciras until after the middle of the century. Still stronger was the Zīrid dynasty in Granada, which shortly after mid-century added Malaga to its domains. About the same time Algeciras and the small towns between it and the Guadalquivir became subject to Seville. The Ṣaqāliba mostly moved eastwards at the breakdown of the central government, and some of their representatives gained power in coastal towns like Almeria, Valencia and Tortosa; but they did not form dynasties like the Berbers.

Among the "Andalusians" the strongest dynasty was that of the ʿAbbādids in Seville. Its founder was the qāḍī or judge Muḥammad ibn-ʿAbbād, who held the supreme power from 1013 to 1042. He was succeeded by his son and grandson, usually known by their honorific titles of al-Muʿtaḍid (1042–68) and al-Muʿtamid (1068–91). Al-Muʿtaḍid greatly extended the small kingdom of Seville to the west and south-west, and engaged in fighting against Cordova and Granada in the east. Cordova was eventually included in his kingdom by al-Muʿtamid. Despite the political upheavals art and letters flourished under the "party kings", since each little ruler imitated the splendour of the former caliphal court as far as his resources permitted. The court of Seville, however, under al-Muʿtaḍid and al-Muʿtamid, was undoubtedly the most brilliant in Spain.[4]

Cordova, after the fall of the ʿĀmirids in 1009, was first of all the chief scene of the struggle for the caliphate. In the course of this it was pitilessly sacked in 1013. Jahwar, the man responsible for the declaration abolishing the caliphate in 1031, virtually held supreme power thereafter, though he tried to insist that rule was in the hands of a council. He was followed by his son and grandson; and historians sometimes speak of a dynasty of Jahwarids.[5] Cordova, as just mentioned, was finally added to the domains of Seville, after a short interlude when it was under Toledo.

The disintegration of al-Andalus was, of course, the opportunity for the Christian princes in the north, and, though occasionally still quarrelling among themselves, they did not fail to make use of the opportunity. Instead of themselves paying tribute to the caliph, they were able to demand tribute from the "party kings". First it was the turn of the rulers on the Marches—at Badajoz, Toledo and Saragossa—to reach this degree of subordination. The most vigorous of the Christian rulers, Alfonso VI of Leon and Castile (1065–1109), was able to exact tribute even from the relatively strong kingdom of Seville. The "party kingdom" of Toledo was the weakest of the three on the Marches and succumbed to Alfonso in 1085. This was an important stage in the Reconquista, since Toledo was never afterwards in Muslim hands. Yet one wonders how far a man like Alfonso was consciously fighting as a Christian against Muslims, and how far simply strengthening his own kingdom. It has been suggested that the Christian Spaniards and the Arabo-Iberian Muslims (called "Andalusians" above) felt themselves to be essentially a single people. One point corroborating this suggestion is the Muslim acceptance of "feudal ideas" (discussed in the previous section). Another illustration would be the career of the Cid; this name is an Arabic title (*sayyid* or *sīd* meaning "lord") which is used *par excellence* of Rodrigo

Diaz de Vivar, a Castilian noble, who about 1081 after a quarrel with Alfonso VI offered his services as a military leader to the Muslim king of Saragossa and ended as independent ruler of the Muslim town of Valencia. Despite his close association with Muslims he was adopted by Christian Spain as a paragon of manly prowess.[6]

The fall of Toledo and the generally threatening situation caused al-Muʿtamid of Seville to seek the help of the ruler of the powerful Almoravid state in North Africa, Yūsuf ibn-Tāshufīn (or Tāshfīn). Yūsuf brought an army across the straits to Spain and defeated Alfonso VI at Zallāqa near Badajoz in 1086; then he and his men returned to Africa. Despite the Muslim victory, however, the threat continued; Yūsuf was again summoned, and arrived in 1088. The campaign did not go so smoothly as he had hoped, and under the influence of the Mālikite jurists of al-Andalus he decided not simply to pursue the limited objectives of those who invited him, but to make an all-out effort on his own account to retrieve the fortunes of Islam. At the end of 1090 he moved forward to dispossess the Muslim rulers, and in the course of 1091 Cordova and Seville fell into his hands. This may be taken as the beginning of the Almoravid period.

(7)

THE BERBER EMPIRES, THE ALMORAVIDS

1. *The Foundations of the Almoravid State*

THE North African state to which the eyes of Spanish Muslims turned after the fall of Toledo in 1085 had grown to a vast size in less than half a century. It included not merely the whole of Morocco and Mauritania, but also the basin of the Senegal river in the south and the western part of Algeria in the north. Only meagre accounts have been preserved of the outward history of the religious movement of the Almoravids, and these give little understanding of the fundamental causes of its rapid success. This is one of many subjects which deserve fuller investigation.[1]

The movement began in a group of camel-breeding, nomadic Berber tribes known collectively as Ṣanhāja. Their home had been the steppes of the Sahara, but some of them had moved south to the basins of the Senegal and the upper Niger. They are the ancestors of the modern Tuareg, and it may be that "Senegal" is derived from their name through a dialectal variant "Ṣanāga". The story of the movement begins with the performance of the pilgrimage to Mecca by some notables of one of the Ṣanhāja tribes, led by their chief Yaḥyā ibn-Ibrāhīm. On their way back they spent some time in Cairouan, then the intellectual centre of North Africa (apart from Egypt). Here they were much impressed by the teaching of a Mālikite jurist, Abū-'Imrān al-Fāsī,[2] who probably died a few months after their visit. He realised how much they and their fellow-tribesmen needed instruction, and with his support they prevailed on the pupil of a pupil of his to accompany them as teacher. The man was Ibn-Yāsīn (more fully, ʿAbd-Allāh ibn-Yāsīn al-Jazūlī), and the date April 1039.

The subdivision of Ṣanhāja to which Yaḥyā ibn-Ibrāhīm belonged did not like the teaching of Ibn-Yāsīn, and at length the latter, with some disciples from another subdivision, retired to an island in the Niger, and is reported to have given himself up to religious studies and pious exercises. European conceptions, however, must not be allowed to mislead us, for despite the undoubted mysticism and asceticism these men presently emerged as fierce and efficient soldiers. The Arabic word for such a "house of retreat" as they had is *ribāṭ*, and from this is derived the usual name of the adherents of Ibn-Yāsīn's movement, al-Murābiṭūn, which has come through Spanish and French into English in the form "Almoravids". These facts help to make it clear that what attracted the Ṣanhāja in the first place was not simply Mālikite jurisprudence, but the mystical teaching associated with it; and it is noteworthy that the man who first stirred the Ṣanhāja, Abū-ʿImrān al-Fāsī, was regarded as a saint by later ṣūfīs or mystics.

It was about the year 1055 that the Almoravid army entered on a phase of expansion by conquering the small state with its capital at the oasis of Sijilmāsa. The military leader here was Yaḥyā ibn-ʿUmar, but Ibn-Yāsīn was still the acknowledged spiritual head. When Yaḥyā was killed a year or so later, Ibn-Yāsīn saw to it that he was succeeded by his brother Abū-Bakr ibn-ʿUmar, and (since Ibn-Yāsīn in turn was killed about 1058) Abū-Bakr remained supreme head (*amīr*) of the movement till his death in 1087. Successes now came rapidly, and in 1061 Abū-Bakr gave his

PLATE 10. Arched entrance to the Sala de los Embajadores in the Alcázar, Seville, Mudejar style.

cousin, Yūsuf ibn-Tāshufīn, a semi-independent command in the northern regions, while he himself devoted his attention to the south. From the new capital of Marrakesh (Marrākush), which he founded in 1062, Yūsuf ibn-Tāshufīn extended Almoravid rule over the fertile areas of Morocco and the western half of modern Algeria.

This expansion of the Almoravids and their growth in power is partly explained by the fact that the regions they conquered were at that period divided up into many small, weak states; but it was presumably the combination of religious and political aims which gave the Almoravids their power by making possible a measure of unity between the various subdivisions of Ṣanhāja. The rapid growth of empires from insignificant beginnings has been a not infrequent feature of nomadic life, and a comparison at once springs to mind with the religious and political movement in Arabia under Muḥammad. Apart from the final outcome, however, there were various differences. One was that the Almoravids found a ready-made system of law, and worked as much as possible through the existing Mālikite jurists. Another was that they acknowledged themselves part of a greater unit by professing loyalty to the ʿAbbāsid caliphs in Baghdad.

2. *The Almoravids in Spain*

Yūsuf ibn-Tāshufīn : (1090)–1106
ʿAlī ibn-Yūsuf : 1106–1143
Tāshufīn ibn-ʿAlī : 1143–1145

Nothing but the desperate situation in which they found themselves after the fall of Toledo in 1085 could have induced al-Muʿtamid of Seville and other rulers in

PLATE 11. Some of the roofs of the Royal Palace of the Alhambra, Granada.

al-Andalus to invite Yūsuf ibn-Tāshufīn to Spain. Before finally concluding an agreement with him they made stipulations about his return to Africa after the hoped-for defeat of the Christians; and he, while accepting these in principle, made some counter-stipulations. Algeciras was eventually given to him as a base, and in late summer 1086 he and his men set out to meet the army of Alfonso VI. The armies met at Zallāqa near Badajoz, and the result was a complete victory for the Muslims; the Christians were either killed or put to flight in disorder. In due course Yūsuf and his men returned to Africa in accordance with his undertakings.

The victory of Zallāqa, however, though a setback for Alfonso VI, did nothing to alter the basic situation in Spain, namely, that the Muslims, because they were so divided (and perhaps for other reasons), were much weaker than the Christians and unable to parry attacks. In particular the eastern coastal regions from Valencia to Lorca were virtually still controlled by Alfonso, and, with a Castilian garrison in the strong fortress of Aledo between Lorca and Murcia, his hold on the region was increasing. Further appeals were therefore made to Yūsuf ibn-Tāshufīn both by the Mālikite jurists and by al-Muʿtamid and other princes. Yūsuf and his captains for their part had tasted something of the luxury of al-Andalus, and were probably not loth to return. In addition they believed that they were promoting the cause of Islam by fighting against its enemies. In the spring of 1090, therefore, Almoravid forces landed for the second time at Algeciras, and Yūsuf led them and the contingents from al-Andalus against the fortress of Aledo. The siege dragged on for several months. When Alfonso VI approached with a relieving army, Yūsuf retired to Lorca, but Alfonso found the fortress to all intents indefensible and razed it to the ground. Yūsuf had thus gained one important objective.

During the siege Yūsuf had also been taking stock of the

general political situation in Spain. He realised that in most of the petty states the control of affairs was in the hands of members of the Arabo-Andalusian aristocracy, and that these persons, though Muslims, were not deeply attached to the Islamic religion but were chiefly interested in poetry, belles-lettres and the arts generally. On the other hand, he was aware that he had a great volume of support from the ordinary people and from the Mālikite jurists. If it may be presumed that he originally intended to retire again to Africa after setting the Muslims of Spain on their feet, it had become clear to him by the closing months of 1090 that this was not feasible. The controlling aristocracies in the petty kingdoms and principalities were too suspicious of one another to be able to resist Alfonso. The interests of the Muslims as a whole called for Yūsuf to unify al-Andalus under himself, and he was presumably moved in the same direction by his own ambitions coupled with the expansionist ethos of the Almoravid polity, of which he was now supreme head.

Yūsuf lost no time in acting on the decision he had taken. Before the end of 1090 he had occupied Granada without fighting. In March 1091 Cordova fell to him, and soon afterwards he began a siege of Seville which led to the surrender of that city and of al-Muʿtamid himself in September. Various smaller towns had also passed under his control. The south of Spain had thus been incorporated into the Almoravid empire, and, as opportunity offered, its grip was extended northwards. The most important stages were the capture of Badajoz in 1094, of Valencia in 1102 and of Saragossa in 1110. In Valencia the Cid had died in 1099, but his widow had been able to maintain independence for some time longer. The fall of Valencia, as also that of the other petty states, was an indication of the great military superiority of the Almoravids over Alfonso. Despite this the Almoravids were not strong enough to occupy any territory that had been effectively occupied by the Christians, who had been pursuing a policy of resettling empty lands with Mozarabic Christians from al-Andalus. In particular the Almoravids were unable to recapture Toledo.

The power of this Berber dynasty did not long remain at its zenith. Generals, other officers and men were filled with admiration for the culture and material luxury of al-Andalus, which far surpassed that of the cities of North Africa and still more that of the steppe environment from which they originally came. This admiration led, if not to moral corruption, at least to a weakening of moral fibre. All began to consider only their own interests, and senior officers lost control of those under them. There was a loss of cohesion in the ruling institution as a whole. Financial difficulties were superimposed on the arrogant behaviour of the Berber soldiery to produce disaffection among sections of the ordinary people; and this disaffection was sufficient to produce a change of fortune for the régime.

The decline began in 1118 with the loss of Saragossa to Alfonso I of Aragon (el Batallador); the disloyalty of much of the populace contributed to this setback. The same Christian king was able to make excursions far into the south of the country in 1125 and 1126, and to remove numbers of Mozarabs for resettlement in newly acquired Christian regions in the north. Alfonso VII of Castile was able to make a similar expedition into the south in 1133. Eventually the growing disaffection and discontent of the common people led to the rebellions of 1144 and 1145 which ended Almoravid rule in Spain.

There is not yet any general agreement among scholars on how to assess Almoravid Spain. The view of Dozy, which has mostly held the field so far, was that Yūsuf ibn-Tāshufīn and his generals were semi-barbarians, and the Mālikite jurists mere narrow-minded bigots, with the result that the sparkle and splendour of the culture of al-Andalus was changed to gloom, while the poets and other writers were denied free expression. There are a number of facts which fit in with this view, but on the whole it appears to be too one-sided,[3] though the point is another of those which require further study. For one thing there is an element of "class war" involved. The dominant class of the previous period, which has here been called the Arabo-Andalusian aristocracy, had lost its power to the Almoravid dynasty collaborating with the Mālikite jurists, and having the favour of the common people (who at first were probably more contented than during the period of party kings). Our information about the Almoravid rule, however, comes mostly from members of the former dominant class—the very class for whom life had become difficult. Yet even if secular poets could find few patrons, the decorative arts are now known to have been flourishing, and the same seems to be true of popular forms of poetry and song.

It would further appear that it was during the Almoravid period that the Muslims of Spain first became fully conscious of the distinctive character of their religion and religious community. Up to this time Spanish Islam had been often, perhaps mostly, a formal and official religion, accepted as a matter of course, but without any burning enthusiasm. Now for many men it became a matter of intense inner conviction. It was doubtless because of this emphasis on Islam as a religion that the jurists made life difficult for Jews and Christians. In part the new awareness of Islam may have been a response to the growing self-awareness of the Christians. Such opposition, too, as there was to poetry and belles-lettres may have been because they were secular and Spanish and not sufficiently Islamic. A large area of common culture was shared by the Christian aristocracies and the Arabo-Andalusian aristocracy. One piece of evidence for this is the readiness of Muslims to remain (under legal safeguards) in the towns where they had lived after these came into the control of the Christians.

After the effective end of Almoravid rule in Spain in 1145, there was a period of much confusion before al-Andalus came to be firmly in the grasp of the Almohads about 1170. These years are sometimes known as the second period of "party kings", but the name is not altogether a happy one. There was indeed a measure of breaking up into small states under "petty kings", but these did not represent "parties" (*ṭawā'if*) as had been the case with the rulers of the small states which appeared when the Umayyad caliphate broke up. After 1145, too, some of the rulers of small states acknowledged the suzerainty of the Almohads, others that of various Christian kings. For the purposes of a survey such as the present it is sufficient to regard the Almohad period as beginning in 1145 with their first intervention in the affairs of al-Andalus.

(8)

THE BERBER EMPIRES, THE ALMOHADS

1. *Ibn-Tūmart and the Almohad Movement*

THERE are various similarities between the Almohad and Almoravid empires. Both came into existence in north-west Africa, and then later included al-Andalus in their territories. Both were ruled by a Berber dynasty, and found their original supporters among Berber tribesmen. Both were in origin religious movements, or, perhaps rather, had a religious basis. It was only natural, of course, that the Berbers, who supported the Almohads, should be the centuries-old enemies of those who supported the Almoravids. The latter were nomads of the group of tribes known as Ṣanhāja, whereas the former were mountaineers from the Atlas belonging to the Maṣmūda. From the scholar's point of view, moreover, there is far more source material about the beginnings of the Almohads than about that of the Almoravids.[1]

The founder of the Almohad movement is commonly known as Ibn-Tūmart (Tūmart being a Berber diminutive of his father's name 'Umar). His family belonged to a branch of the tribe of Hintāta, and he was born in a village in the Atlas in the years round about 1082. As a student he visited Cordova, then went east to Alexandria, Mecca and Baghdad. It is doubtful whether he heard lectures from the great intellectual leader of the time, al-Ghazālī; but he probably learnt something of the philosophical theology known as Ash'arism in the Niẓāmiyya college at Baghdad and in Alexandria. In the course of his studies and travels he became filled with reforming zeal. As a basis for his reforms, however, he had elaborated Islamic dogma in a new form. In this much emphasis was placed on *taw'ḥīd*, "unity" or rather "assertion of unity", and as a result his followers came to be known as al-Muwaḥḥidūn, "the assertors of unity", or (in European languages) Almohads or Almohades.

Ibn-Tūmart's enthusiasm led him to commence preaching to the crew and passengers of the ship from Alexandria, and then to the inhabitants of the towns through which he passed. The results were not altogether promising. Sometimes violent opposition was roused, and Ibn-Tūmart had to leave hurriedly. It was after his expulsion from Bougie (Bijāya) in 1117 or 1118 that Ibn-Tūmart met the man who was to carry the movement to political success, 'Abd-al-Mu'min. The latter was himself a student and had had thoughts of going east, but from this time onward he remained attached to Ibn-Tūmart. After spending some time in Marrakesh, where there was the usual mixture of support and opposition, they withdrew to the comparative solitude of the remote town of Tinmelal (Tīnmāl, etc.). This became a centre of propaganda for the new doctrine, which rapidly gained supporters and was given a hierarchical organisation.[2] About 1121 Ibn-Tūmart put forward the claim to be himself the Mahdī, the divinely guided and inspired leader. Soon he had sufficient men under him to challenge Almoravid power at the local level. A defeat in 1023 did not halt his progress. He himself was military as well as spiritual leader, and found his death in battle in 1130.

Ibn-Tūmart had designated 'Abd-al-Mu'min as his successor, but it was not until 1133 that the latter was proclaimed. At first he had to confine himself to guerrilla tactics, but eventually he gained sufficient support in the mountainous regions to venture into the plains to meet the main Almoravid armies. He had somewhat the better of an encounter near Tlemcen in 1145, and soon after the battle the Almoravid ruler died as the result of an accident. The ensuing weakness of the Almoravid administration led in 1147 to the loss of their capital Marrakesh and the establishment of the Almohads there. This was to all intents and purposes the end of the Almoravid state.

Though ʿAbd-al-Mu'min had interfered in al-Andalus as early as 1145, he did not direct his main military effort after 1147 to taking over the Almoravid domains there, but was content with diplomatic activities. He had realised that there were opportunities for expanding eastwards in Africa far beyond the limits reached by the Almoravids. Here, however, there was a Christian threat to be met, namely, from Roger II of Sicily. Nevertheless, the eastern half of modern Algeria fell to him as the result of a carefully prepared campaign in 1151, while a further campaign in 1159–60 gave him Tunisia including the towns of Tunis, Cairouan and al-Mahdiyya (the former Fāṭimid capital), and the coast of North Africa as far east as Tripoli.

2. *Spain under the Almohads (to 1223)*

ʿAbd-al-Mu'min : 1130–1163
Abū-Yaʿqūb Yūsuf I : 1163–1184
Abū-Yūsuf Yaʿqūb al-Manṣūr : 1184–1199
Muhammad an-Nāṣir : 1199–1213
Abū-Yaʿqūb Yūsuf II : 1213–1223

The position of al-Andalus after the loss of control by the Almoravids in 1145, and still more after the Almohad capture of Marrakesh in 1147, is obscure. Effective power was in the hands of a number of petty local rulers. Some of these may for a time have continued to be, in some respects, dependent on the Christian kings, but more and more they tended to acknowledge the suzerainty of the Almohad caliph. The greatest measure of independence was shown by Ibn-Mardanīsh who ruled Seville and had some control over much of the west of al-Andalus.

The founder of the Almohad empire, 'Abd-al-Mu'min, after incorporating Tunisia and Tripolitania, began to think once more of the Iberian peninsula and from 1162 was making preparations for a large-scale campaign there. Before the plans could come to fruition his death intervened, and the son who (after a short dispute) succeeded him, Abū-Ya'qūb Yūsuf, did not carry out these plans. It was not indeed until 1171 that the new caliph attempted to take a firmer grip of al-Andalus. There was opposition from Ibn-Mardanīsh, but his death in 1172 left his successors with little choice except to surrender Seville to the Almohads. The caliph proceeded northwards after this, and for a time besieged Toledo; but eventually he realised the great difficulty of the operation and his folly in prosecuting this enterprise, and therefore abandoned it. After this, however, the Almohads seem to have had effective control of most of al-Andalus. In a later campaign Abū-Ya'qūb Yūsuf was able to carry the "holy war" into the enemy's territory. Unfortunately he was wounded in besieging the fortress of Santarem (near Lisbon), and shortly afterwards died from his wound (1184).

The first task of his son and successor, Abū-Yūsuf Ya'qūb, was to recover the town of Bougie and the neighbouring part of the Algerian littoral from a descendant of the Almoravids who had set himself up there as an independent ruler. This series of events shows that, though the Almohads could bring together, when it was required, an extremely powerful army, the forces by which they maintained order in normal times were insufficient to restrain adventurers. There was usually thus some part of his empire which needed the special attention of the Almohad caliph. It was not until 1189 that Abū-Yūsuf Ya'qūb was able to give attention of this kind to al-Andalus. Various successes enabled him to get the agreement of the kings of Castile and Leon to a five years' truce in 1190. After further operations against fortresses in Portugal in the same year and the following one, he was able to leave al-Andalus in a comparatively settled condition while he attended to urgent matters in Africa. The end of the truce led to a further period of activity in the Iberian peninsula. Early in the campaign in July 1195 the Almohads won a great victory over Alfonso VIII of Castile at Alarcos (about half-way between Cordova and Toledo). The victory was partly exploited then and in the following year, but the Almohads seem to have lacked the resources to bring about any fundamental change in the balance of power between Christian Spain and al-Andalus.

The Christians, on the other hand, were goaded into increased activity by this reverse, which came precisely at the time when they thought the reconquest was moving smoothly forward. Bishops and archbishops played an active part in ironing out the differences between political leaders, patching up quarrels, and removing mutual suspicions. A crusade was preached not only in Spain but also beyond the Pyrenees, and this brought many reinforcements. These preparations were made easier by the truce which was signed after the battle of Alarcos, and by the lack of vigour of the new Almohad caliph, Muḥammad, who succeeded to his father in 1199. For a time the situation was stable, with the Almohad dominion in Spain apparently at its zenith; but when the Christians eventually moved to the offensive it was soon obvious that a decisive shift had taken place in the balance of power. It was in July 1212 that a combined force from Leon, Castile, Navarre and Aragon moved south from Toledo and met the Almohads at Las Navas de Tolosa. The Almohads suffered such a defeat that their power in Spain was virtually broken for good and all, though this did not become manifest till after

1223 owing to the Christians being once again distracted by internal problems. The caliph Muḥammad died, perhaps accidentally, in 1213, and his son of fifteen who succeeded him, Abū-Yaʿqūb Yūsuf II, was incapable of restoring the fortunes of the tottering régime.

It would be interesting to know the reasons for the Almohad debacle, but the matter has received little consideration, and anything that may be said here must be of a tentative nature. There are a few points, however, that are relatively certain. Ibn-Tūmart had grown up in the Almoravid empire, and from one point of view his doctrines are seen to be directed against the Almoravids. The Almoravid régime was closely linked with the Mālikite jurists for whom jurisprudence meant knowledge of the details of law as applied in practice, that is, knowledge of what recognised authorities had decided. Ibn-Tūmart, however, held that the jurist must be able to derive his decisions about the application of the law from first principles, that is, from actual texts in the Qur'ān and the Traditions, or from the consensus of the Muslims. Another important matter was Ibn-Tūmart's claim to be the Mahdī (the divinely-sent leader and restorer of order). Though this was a Shīʿite rather than a Sunnite belief, Ibn-Tūmart was doubtless thinking not of any tie-up with the Shīʿites in the east, but of providing a focus for the deep-seated Berber reverence for saints and holy men (of which the popular respect for marabouts is evidence).

A régime with a dogmatic basis of this kind was bound to oppose the class of Mālikite jurists who had had so much influence under the Almoravids. Yet they do not seem to have provided themselves with any alternative body of jurists, though some of those who supported them were Ẓāhirites (cf. p. 130f. below). Elsewhere Shīʿite leaders like the Fāṭimids claimed to be able to give authoritative decisions on points of law, though they seldom in practice produced any extensive legal novelties. Ibn-Tūmart does not even seem to have claimed so much. On certain points he insisted on a strict carrying out of the prescriptions of the Qur'ān and the Traditions, but in general he seems to have been content with the law as currently administered. Thus there was no basic conflict between the new doctrines and current legal practice such as to exclude the existing jurists automatically. The Almohads did indeed claim the title of caliph for themselves, and abandoned even the formal acknowledgement of the 'Abbāsids in Baghdad; but the Mālikite jurists were presumably not greatly concerned about the 'Abbāsids. More and more, then, the corps of Mālikite jurists continued to exercise their functions under the Almohads in al-Andalus.

The further fact that the Almohads had at times to make concessions in order to retain the goodwill of the jurists is perhaps a pointer to the most serious weakness of the Almohads—the lack of popular support. The Almoravids had removed the old Arabo-Andalusian aristocracy from power and found their support in the Mālikite jurists and the common people. The Almohads may to some extent have had active support from the dispossessed aristocracy; but they had little from the populace once the momentary feeling of relief from Almoravid abuses had passed. The figure of the Mahdī which had appealed to the Berbers had probably little attraction for the inhabitants of al-Andalus, just as it may have had little attraction for the Arabs in the eastern regions of the Almohad empire in North Africa. If this is so, it means that the Almohad empire was first and foremost a military state requiring only the minimum degree of consent from the persons ruled. There was no enthusiasm among the people, and no sense of being associated with the ruling élite in a momentous cause. In the difficult days after 1223 at least one member of the ruling family abandoned his allegiance to the doctrines of Ibn-Tūmart; so the state of affairs among the rank and file may be imagined. This more than anything else seems to have brought about the decline of the Almohad régime.

A contributory factor was doubtless the Berber origin of the ruling élite. This meant that the figure of al-Mahdī had probably little attraction for the non-Berber Muslims of al-Andalus; the basic hope of the native Iberian stock seems to have been for direct supernatural intervention.[3] Again, there was apparently an embryonic form of national or racial awareness, perhaps chiefly for linguistic reasons. The Almohads were at first successful in gaining the allegiance of the numerous Arabs in eastern Algeria and Tunisia; but it would be only natural if, after a time, the differing fundamental orientations of the linguistic groups caused political repercussions.

3. *The Progress of the Reconquista from 1223 to 1248*

The Almohad caliph who died in 1223 left no son, and dynastic quarrels ensued which virtually ended resistance to the Reconquista in al-Andalus with one exception. In North Africa, despite the quarrels within the ruling family, something of the Almohad empire continued to exist, but it was gradually whittled away as subordinates made themselves independent and new states were established, until it became finally extinct in 1269. In al-Andalus some of the Almohad rulers retained a measure of authority in limited areas for a few years after 1223, but the central administration had disappeared.

In this period of confusion a descendant of former princes of Saragossa seemed for a time to be gaining a notable measure of success in the east and south of al-Andalus. After the union of Leon and Castile in 1230, however, the Christians once more took the offensive, and he was defeated more than once in battle and finally assassinated. After this no single Muslim leader had much support, though some preserved a precarious measure of semi-independence for two or three decades. The leader of the Christian offensive was Ferdinand III, king of Castile from 1217 and of Leon also from 1230 (until his death in 1252). In a series of campaigns from 1231 onwards he finally conquered for the Christians the very heart of al-Andalus. The outstanding events were the occupation of Cordova in 1236 and of Seville in 1248. After that "mopping-up operations", especially in the east, may be said to have taken twenty years. By the end of this period Muslim rule in Spain had disappeared with one exception.

The one exception—the one gleam of light for the Muslims—was the appearance of the Naṣrid kingdom of Granada. About 1231 a man of Arab descent (from Medina), Muḥammad ibn-Yūsuf ibn-Naṣr, founded a little state for himself round Jaén, and then in 1235 seized Granada and made it his capital. He kept his head above water by careful diplomacy—getting Christian help against local Muslim rivals, and then North African Muslim help against the Christians. The geographical features of this small kingdom, together with other factors, enabled it to maintain itself for two and a half centuries.

Apart from this small, though important exception, however, the fall of the Almohads meant the end of Islamic Spain.

(9)
CULTURAL GREATNESS IN POLITICAL DECLINE

1. *Poetry*

THE poetry which under the Spanish Umayyads had been establishing itself in new soil, growing and building up energy, burst into flower in the late tenth and the eleventh centuries. This was a period of political division and instability, but poetry does not immediately rise and fall with every fluctuation of political fortune, and the fact that under the "party kings" there were several courts, each rivalling the others in the patronage of arts, gave scope for many poets to prove their talents and reap their rewards.

There was no lack of talent. The most celebrated of all Andalusian poets was Ibn-Zaydūn (1003–70) who expressed with much tenderness and delicacy his unhappy love for the princess Wallāda, herself a poetess. The severe theologian Ibn-Ḥazm (994–1064) also composed a treatise on love, *The Ring of the Dove*, illustrating each of the aspects of love and the experiences of lovers with verses by himself and by others. Particularly distinguished was the court of the ʿAbbādids in Seville, where the tone was set by princes who were themselves gifted poets, by al-Muʿtaḍid (1012–69), a poet of vigorous spirit capable at his best of coining some striking similes, and even more by his son al-Muʿtamid (1040–95). Al-Muʿtamid gave fine expression

PLATE 12. Slender columns in the Patio de los Leones at the Alhambra, Granada.

to the fashionable themes of his time before he was reduced to abject captivity by the Almoravids, and poured out his heart in pathetic laments. In his service also was a close friend whom he advanced to high office but who eventually fell out of favour and was put to death, Ibn-ʿAmmār (1031–83), whose verses have a certain grandeur and resonance; and to his court came Ibn-Ḥamdīs (1055–1132) when driven out of Sicily by the Normans.

This golden age of Andalusian poetry is generally held to have come to an end with the eleventh century, and this is true in the sense that no significant new upsurge took place thereafter; but the models then created continued to be imitated with great skill and refinement for several centuries. Fine poets continued to thrive under the Berber dynasties, not least in the provinces, the most distinguished being Ibn Khafāja of Alcira (1050–1139), particularly renowned for his descriptions of gardens.

It is tempting to connect this flowering of poetry with life in the secular, tolerant principalities of the Reyes de Taifas, "turbaned Italian republics" as they have been dubbed, or rather with the leisure of their courts. It is also easy to ascribe its subsequent loss of vitality to the reactionary and repressive character of the Berber dynasties, whose rulers are often depicted as semi-barbarians incapable of appreciating the subtleties of the Andalusian mind. There is indeed a measure of truth in these assertions, but against their unqualified acceptance must be set the facts that life under the "party kings" was not without its seamy side of base intrigue and gnawing insecurity, that the successors of Yūsuf ibn-Tāshufīn were quick to adopt Andalusian attitudes and offer their patronage to poets, and that poetry did not in fact significantly alter its character as one dynasty succeeded another.

PLATE 13. Detail of stucco on the walls of the Patio de los Leones at the Alhambra, Granada.

No more in this age than in any other can poetry be neatly explained in terms of political and social conditions. With perhaps nothing more precise to stimulate it than the bounty of nature and the Umayyad Caliphate's patronage and promise of grandeur, Andalusian poetry developed along lines that quickly became stylized, and its life was thus protracted even when very different times had come not only upon Spain but upon the whole of Islam, times when three Caliphates had gone into decline, when enemies were threatening from without and orthodoxy was reacting within.[1]

It is in fact difficult to imagine any society where the distinctive poetry of al-Andalus could for long be anything but a conventional or escapist expression. Its main themes were those of fastidious, luxurious pleasure-seeking. Other themes honoured in Arabic literature—the gnomic, the ascetic, the mystic—did have their spokesmen, but they were in poor voice. Instead, we read of drinking parties held on the river at night, or in a grove or flowery meadow either in the cool of the evening or at dawn "when night washes off its *kohl* in the morning dew"; of fawn-like ephebes or girls slim-waisted and round-hipped inducing inebriation by the wine they pour, by the glances they give, by the kisses they yield; while to the accompaniment of a lute a slave-girl sings or another dances, finally slipping out of her dress to appear "like a bud unfolding from a cluster of blossoms".[2]

There was refinement as well as sensuality in these pleasures. The Andalusian poets showed minute and lively care in every object of beauty, and the ideal expressed by Ibn-Khafāja was not of a man so sturdy or stoic or staid as never to lose a night's sleep because of love, but of one reacting immediately to every stimulus, angered or depressed by adversity, but also trembling with joy at the sight of beauty, "like the branch of a ben-tree wet with dew, which the blowing of a gentle breeze bends this way and that".[3] This refined sensuality is manifested in the special interest that Andalusian poets took in nature and in love.

Nature provided the idyllic background for bacchic scenes and lovers' meetings, but it was then only vaguely sketched in. It was usually single items that came in for minute observation—dusk, the wavelets on the surface of the river, and especially single flowers, the description of which was so popular that it filled some anthologies and was recognised as a genre on its own. Flowers especially were often somewhat artificially depicted as arrangements of gems—the nenuphar as white pearls with a black bead in the centre, the wild jasmine on its green stem as a yellow hyacinth on an emerald rod; but there were also comparisons of great variety and ingenuity, often involving personification, the flowing river being seen as the tremulous flanks of a thinly clad dancer, the night as a negro king with the moon for a diadem and Gemini for ear-rings. Nor did Andalusian poets fail to project emotion into nature, sensing in the cooing of doves and the sighing of the breeze expressions of sympathy with parted lovers.

In love-poetry too the Andalusians ranged very widely, from consuming passion to dalliance, from expressions of abject submission to one's mistress to mock adjudication on compensation due for the wounds of love, from the uncomplicated sensuality of an Ibn-Khafāja—

> My hands travelled about his body
> Now to the waist and now to the breast,
> Descending to the Tihāma of his flanks
> And rising to the Najd of his breasts.[4]

—to Ibn-Ḥazm's protestation that he preferred to meet his beloved in a dream lest in reality the touch of his hand should make her fade away.[5]

Yet the range does not extend significantly beyond the sensual, no matter how refined. In *The Ring of the Dove*

Ibn-Ḥazm did reflect the (ultimately Neoplatonic) view that love is the reunion of the two halves of a spirit created as one sphere, but the recognition was always through physical attraction. "Platonic" love in this context is related to a peculiar psychology of ambiguous chastity, whereby the erotic orientation was a morbid perpetuation of desire[6] since, in physical love, fulfilment and satiety must coincide. Woman is said to have had much freedom and to have been much exalted in Andalusian society, but in poetry it was always her physical charms that were sung, the only character trait mentioned—though chastity in the man was sometimes praised—being her caprice and cruelty in denying her lover. One passage is quoted by Henri Pérès[7] in which ar-Raḍī, the son of al-Muʿtamid, told his beloved: "Thou art beautiful both physically and morally" but it is also a passage in which occurred a striking—and rare—indication of Christian influence, for the beloved was also spoken of as "an angel".

The question is thus raised of a possible kinship between certain attitudes observable in Andalusian and in European literatures. Pérès more than any other has meticulously examined the poetic production of the eleventh century. He has made much of instances of personification of nature as against the Arab tendency to de-animate discussed in earlier chapters. He has seen as distinctive a number of features of which he judges the fundamental one to be: a love of nature which, despite some artificiality of expression, is rooted in reality; and an underlying melancholy which gives the Andalusian poets a preference for half-tints. They prefer spring to summer, evening and night to noon. Even when they are among boon companions, one feels they prefer silence and solitude. Perhaps because of the instability of life, they feel that no pleasures are wholly pure, and "a disquiet—rare among Orientals—troubles every act that is a tribute to life". Their humble attitude to woman and their conception of love are almost Christian.

All in all, "for the virtues of strength and of action—which constitute the fitting ideal of Arab society in Islam—they substitute qualities of mildness, of humility, of tenderness, of reflectiveness and of musing. They tend to become more fully human by developing all faculties, by allowing, perhaps, precedence to the heart over the mind and will."

Indeed Pérès sees in the Andalusians such a preponderance of Ibero-Roman blood as to make them, despite the presence of undeniably Oriental elements, a continuation of the aboriginal people; and to the Judaeo-Christian element he ascribes a major role in the development of their distinctive features.[8]

Impressive and instructive as Pérès' study is, it is difficult to agree with his conclusions, or at least with the weight he gives to the distinctiveness of Andalusian poetry. Substantially, this poetry is one with that of the Islamic East. The Andalusians never lost their interest in the literary production of the East. Their habit of characterising their own poets as "the Mutanabbī" or "the Ibn-ar-Rūmī of the West" indicates deference to the standards of the East; Ibn-Ḥazm even complained that he would have been better appreciated if he had not been born in Spain. In fact, Andalusian themes all grew naturally out of classical poetry, and very few of the features singled out by Pérès are without echo elsewhere in Islam. In expression also the Andalusians yielded to none in their search for *recherché* images. The taste for rhetorical word-play was so deeply ingrained that when al-Muʿtamid, languishing in fetters, heard that two of his sons had been killed, it was in bitter puns on their names that he gave voice to his undoubtedly genuine grief. And in the search for ever more extravagant ways of expression, neither artificiality nor bad taste were always avoided, so that a poet as refined and discriminating as Abū ʿĀmir ibn-Shuhayd (992–1035) could yet write:

> Such was my kissing, such my sucking of his mouth that he was almost made toothless.

Yet the distinctive lyricism is there, and has been sensed by many since Baron MacGuckin de Slane remarked on it;[9] but it lies in the preponderance of certain themes, in emotional overtones, perhaps also in a somewhat greater cohesion of mood and homogeneity of imagery, as in Ibn-Khafāja's magnificent description of a lofty and forbidding mountain[10] or in these lines on a party of horsemen, in which all the metaphors are derived from water:

On coursiers like torrent courses did they ride, and tied
To their dun lances the likes of clear blue waters;
Into their scabbards they deposited streams; and chose
For helms, bubbles out of the foam;
They were clad in coats of mail that were pools
Quivering—except over their shoulders.[11]

What is significant is that where Andalusian literary practice diverges from that of the East, it moves in a direction acceptable to European taste.

Miscegenation does not by itself explain this phenomenon, and as has already been seen the Muslim conquerors did not find in Spain an advanced culture worthy of imitation. But the indigenous population had at least a folk-literature, and in the society that evolved—a society which could maintain few barriers between *muwallads* and Mozarabs who were often close kinsmen, a society that had so adapted itself to the co-existence of different cultures that, despite different calendars, some popular Muslim festivals were made to coincide with Christian holidays—this folk-literature must have mingled and fused with that of the newcomers. There is in fact a thirteenth-century text which asserts that the early Andalusians sang "either in the manner of the Nazarenes, or in that of the Arab camel-drivers".[12] It is not difficult to imagine that once hybridisation had taken place at the popular level some of the attitudes that ran through the original folk-literature worked themselves by osmosis even into the convention-ridden compositions of the élite.[13]

Some such process is particularly likely in the development of the strophic forms of poetry, the *muwashshaḥ* and the *zajal*, which are the undisputedly original contribution of al-Andalus to Arabic poetry. The *muwashshaḥ* in its commonest form is a poem of five or more stanzas, with an initial couplet which may have been used as a refrain but which in any case provided a recurring element, in that each stanza thereafter would consist of three lines with a rhyme of their own followed by two lines reproducing the rhyme of the initial couplet. The rhyme scheme would thus be:

AA bbbAA(*AA*)   cccAA(*AA*) etc.

but many elaborations and variations of this scheme were also worked out. The final couplet, called the *kharja*, was to be the "punch line" of the entire poem, and early sources on the theory of *muwashshaḥ* specify that it ought to be composed first, but it could also be borrowed. Again according to these early sources, the *kharja* ought to be snappy and spicy, and ought to be composed not in classical Arabic but in the colloquial idiom or in Romance. In recent years, some such *kharjas* have in fact been discovered; they are in a mixture of colloquial and Romance, and almost always in the form of words put into the mouth of a woman.

The *zajal* is entirely in the colloquial, and usually has a simpler rhyme scheme, with a single line at the end of each stanza reproducing the rhyme of the initial couplet—i.e.:

AA bbbA(*AA*) etc.[14]

Some Andalusian *muwashshaḥs* were composed in metres identical, or nearly so, with those of classical Arabic poetry. Some on the other hand struck Ibn-Sanā'-al-Mulk (d. 1212)—the propagator of the genre in the East—as having, *when read*, no metre that the ear could detect[15] although presumably when sung they were made to fit into a rhythmic pattern by arbitrary contraction or lengthening of the syllables. Between these two extremes are many that can be scanned in accordance with a syllabic system possibly derived from the quantitative classical metres, but noticeably different from them; they raise intriguing problems on which the last word has yet to be said.[16]

The *muwashshaḥ* and the *zajal* are but two of a number of non-classical verse-forms which came to be used in Arabic-speaking lands.[17] One of these at least—the *mawāliyā*—is known to have been practised in Iraq as early as the eighth century A.D. There are also strophic compositions ascribed to the Baghdad poets Abu-Nuwās (d. *c.* 803) and Ibn-al-Muʿtazz (d. 908) which it is not impossible to regard as forerunners of the *muwashshaḥ*.[18] There is no positive evidence, however, that these solitary examples served as models for any later poets. Certainly in the East the development of strophic poetry remained very largely confined to folk-literature until the Andalusians brought the *muwashshaḥ* and the *zajal* to the point where they excited the admiration and then the emulation of cultured Muslims elsewhere, so that the pre-eminence of al-Andalus in this field is uncontested.

The earliest known Andalusian *muwashshaḥs* are from the eleventh century, but their "invention" is ascribed to a poet of Cabra who died early in the tenth. "Invention" here need mean no more than that this poet was first to give the *muwashshaḥ* a form acceptable to men of letters, for the character of the *kharja* bespeaks a popular origin—possibly songs sung by native women entertainers before Arabic-speaking audiences. García Gómez has shown how an Arab poet whose ear had caught a snappy line from a popular song might well have written the first *muwashshaḥ* as a setting for it,[19] but it seems likely that the indebtedness of this poet must have been more extensive, so different is the entire structure of the *muwashshaḥ* from that of classical Arabic poems.

The genre acquired a great vogue, and was practised by many of the best poets, some—like Abū-Bakr Muḥammad ibn-Zuhr (d. 1110/1)—building their literary reputations on their mastery of it. It lent itself well to the prevailing taste for artifice. At the same time, with the stanza rather than the line as its unit, its patterns both adaptable and challenging, the form produced, when handled by masters, some of the most charming of Andalusian love-poems and some of the most delicate descriptive pieces.

Zajal did not make its appearance until quite late, and its principal exponent Ibn-Quzmān or Abenguzman (d. 1160 or 1169)[20] claimed most of the credit for having perfected it. That is not to say that it had not had a lengthy history before then: as a truly popular form, it would have been beneath the attention of the men of letters who might have recorded it. Ibn-Quzmān was the first whose verve and coarse good humour earned him acceptance among men of letters, and hence into posterity.

So it was that in Spain, alone among Muslim lands, the vigorous spirit of the common people breached the wall of convention erected by the classicists.

2. *Prose Literature and Philology*

Linguistic and literary studies have always been particularly closely related in Arabic. The earliest grammarians and lexicographers sought to establish what early, pure Arab usage was, and for this purpose their raw material was the poetry of the Ancients, so that their works were studded with citations used not only in illustration but as authority. Indeed it was they who stimulated the recording of such poetry, and it was an extension and development of their interests that led to the compilation of anthologies, the collection of literary anecdotes, the writing of commentaries on literary texts, the growth of literary criticism itself.

The Muslims in Spain apparently had a distinct educational system—a more rational one than that of the East, as Pérès has been quick to point out[21]—whereby the language was mastered first and the religious "sciences" studied afterwards. But the "sciences" themselves were very much in the tradition of the East. They were first brought over, as has been mentioned, by such learned men as ʿal-Qālī, and the link was maintained by a constant traffic of scholars and of scholarly works, a two-way traffic that emphasises the essential unity of Islamic culture.

Thus Arab grammarians in al-Andalus as elsewhere made their contributions to a common fund of knowledge by writing commentaries on standard works composed in the East. The lexicographer Ibn-Sīda (1006?–66) compiled among other works two great dictionaries of no small renown alike in the East and in the West.

Books of *adab*—collections of miscellaneous items often quite encyclopaedic in their range, for the genre embraced everything of interest to the cultured man—were produced in Spain. One entitled *The Light of Kings* (Sirāj al-Mulūk) by Abū Bakr aṭ-Ṭurṭūshī, also known as Ibn-Abī-Randaqa (1059–1130), consists almost entirely of anecdotes on royal behaviour, and could perhaps be assigned to the special class of "mirrors for princes". Another by Yūsuf ibn-ash-Shaykh of Malaga (1132–1207) dealt with a wide variety of subjects in alphabetical order, and came to be used as a manual of general culture.

There also began to appear anthologies where Andalusian poets had pride of place, and in particular anthologies on a single theme often reflecting the Andalusians' delight in nature; the earliest now extant is Abū-'l-Walīd al-Ḥimyarī's (1026–c. 1084), which is concerned entirely with spring and with spring flowers. Ibn-Ḥazm's *The Ring of the Dove*, already mentioned as an anthology of poetry and in fact inspired by an Eastern anthology, Abū-Dāwud al-Iṣfahānī's *Kitāb az-Zahra*, is at the same time a treatise on love of some considerable originality and of unsurpassed reputation.

It was with the declared aim of doing full justice to Andalusian genius and of breaking away from the subservience to Eastern models that Ibn-Bassām (d. 1147) composed his literary history, well-named *The Treasury* (Adh-Dhakhīra), for it is to this day one of our richest treasure houses of literary information. A younger contemporary, al-Fat'ḥ ibn-Khāqān, drew heavily upon *The Treasury* in his two literary histories, which have nevertheless earned themselves a distinguished reputation for the excellence of their prose style. Finally, not out of rivalry with the East but in response to a Berber challenge issued at the court of the Almohad ruler al-Manṣūr, ash-Shaqundī (d. 1231) composed an Epistle (*Risāla*) in defence of Andalusian culture remarkable for its measured argumentation, its acumen, and its elevated style.

Although the stylistic excellence of both al-Fat'ḥ ibn-Khāqān and ash-Shaqundī has been noted, fine prose as such—prose aimed primarily at creating aesthetic effect rather than conveying information—was a literary activity that grew out of official correspondence. The secretaries of princes were no mere amanuenses, but senior "civil servants", men of responsibility and prestige whose skill with words was deemed not unworthy of the attention of literary critics.

Eventually prose writing was extended beyond official correspondence to epistles on various themes, descriptive pieces, imaginary debates between the sword and the pen or between various kinds of flowers.

Once again, the trail had been blazed in the East, where a number of writers—of whom the most gifted was al-Jāḥiẓ (d. 869)—had developed a lively and direct style of prose; these had their admirers and imitators in al-Andalus. The most renowned was the poet Ibn-Zaydūn: his two epistles—one, written when he was in disgrace, pleading for the ruler's clemency; the other, addressed to his rival Ibn-ʿAbdūs, in satirical vein—are fine pieces of craftsmanship, vigorous, and full of learned allusions.

Before long, the taste for rhetorical artifice had invaded prose as well as poetry. In East and West alike, a cleverly ornate rhymed prose, aimed at commanding the reader's admiration rather than engaging his sympathetic emotions, became the rule in all writing laying claim to literary distinction.

This kind of prose found a particularly suitable outlet in the *maqāma*. This was a short story told with consummate if self-conscious artistry, almost always of a fraud perpetrated by a witty and likeable rogue to secure a free meal or some other modest prize. It was reputedly invented in the East by Badīʿ-az-Zamān al-Hamadhānī (969–1008), but once again the statement need mean no more than that he was the first to give it a polished literary expression. The form and the name of the *maqāma*[22] are consistent with its having grown out of a kind of anecdote which in the ninth century told of some beduin, chaste of speech and austere of manner, haranguing an assembly of notables on the pristine virtues threatened by a life of luxury, but which a century later had reduced the hero to the role of an uninvited guest insinuating himself among his betters to cadge a meal.

Badīʿ-az-Zamān displayed some ingenuity and finesse in the frauds he related, and some lively observation of human behaviour; but his own interest was in the opportunities the *maqāma* offered for fine diction and clever expression, and it is to these that the genre owed its success. Al-Ḥarīrī of Basra (1054–1122) went further in that his hero hardly ever used any means other than his eloquence to bemuse and then to dupe his audience; the narrative thus became no more than a slender frame for verbal *tours de force* of breath-taking brilliance.

The writings of Badīʿ-az-Zamān—epistles as well as

maqāmas—were quickly known, much admired, and soon imitated in Spain. No less favoured were those of al-Ḥarīrī, which some Andalusians are reported to have heard from the lips of the author himself; it was in fact an Andalusian, Abū-'l-ʿAbbās Aḥmad ash-Sharīshī—i.e. of Jerez—(d. 1222) whose commentary on the *maqāmas* of al-Ḥarīrī came to be accepted as the standard one throughout Islam. *Maqāmas* are known to have been composed in al-Andalus from the late eleventh century onward, probably the outstanding contributor to the genre being Abū-'ṭ-Ṭāhir Muḥammad at-Tamīmī as-Saraqusṭī al-Ashtarkūnī—i.e. of Estercuel—(d. 1143), who in the composition of his fifty *maqāmas* imposed upon himself onerous arbitrary standards of verbal ornamentation, apparently in emulation of what the Eastern poet Abū-'l-ʿAlā' al-Maʿarrī (973–1057) had done in his *Luzūmiyyāt*.[23]

Concerned as it is less with a story to be told than with a writer's virtuosity, the *maqāma* is nevertheless—if we except the short anecdote—the only narrative form developed in Arabic literature, prose or verse. An early translation of the fables of Bidpai by the Persian Ibn-al-Muqaffaʿ (d. 757) had gained acceptance as a literary classic. Persian tales in a translation of similarly high quality appear to have formed the core of the *Arabian Nights*, but the anonymity and indifferent language of the later accretions bespeak a popular origin. The masters of Arabic prose in fact left story-telling almost entirely to the common people, and it is consistent with the atomism already noted in Arab literary practice that though they polished their means of expression to a diamond brilliance, they evolved no epic and—until modern times—no drama and no novel, no genre requiring sustained invention in accordance with a unified conception. The one exception of note in the East has been a prose work by the poet al-Maʿarrī, the *Risālat al-Ghufrān* (*The Epistle of Forgiveness*) describing a visit to heaven and encounters there with poets of previous ages; its superficial similarities with the *Divine Comedy* have attracted incidental attention in the debate on whether Dante owed any part of his inspiration to Islamic sources.[24]

In Muslim Spain, the picture was not substantially different. Tales and legends—some of which have been preserved—were part of the heritage of the common people, and these, unhampered by any conscious attachment to a hidebound tradition, freely picked threads from whatever lore offered delight and instruction, threads of Arab or Greek or local origin, and as freely wove them into the patterns suggested by their cross-fertilised imagination. But no literary narrative developed, although one Ibn-al-Kinānī, an eleventh-century physician, was the author of a book entitled *Muḥammad wa-Suʿdā*, now lost, but which would appear to have been some kind of a romance.

There are, however, two Andalusian works of the greatest interest in this connection, even though the narrative element in both was of secondary importance in the author's mind.

The first is the *Risālat at-Tawābiʿ wa-'z-Zawābiʿ* by Abū-ʿĀmir ibn-Shuhayd (992–1035). In this the author describes a journey in supernatural realms where he meets the *tawābiʿ*, the genii (jinn) who—according to pre-Islamic belief—inspired and were individually attached to poets. He has interviews with the genii of three pre-Islamic poets and a number of "moderns". In most instances there is no more than a brief dialogue in which the particular *tābiʿ* hears, usually with approval, an ode after the manner of his own poet but composed by Ibn-Shuhayd. But there are also passages which trace the use made by successive poets of particular conceits and figures of speech; and the book ends with a discussion of the merits of poetic compositions by a mule and by an ass, and with a discourse by a goose—possibly satires on unidentified literary personalities.

This is the first book of the kind known in Arabic, for it

ante-dates by a few years al-Maʿarrī's *Risālat al-Ghufrān*, although there is nothing to show that al-Maʿarrī knew of it. Pérès has suggested[25] that it was itself possibly inspired by some of the *Dialogues* of Plato or of Lucian, but of this again there is no positive evidence. It is at all events primarily literary criticism presented in fanciful form. Nevertheless the story is told with some verve, at times with a tongue-in-the-cheek humour rare indeed in Arabic literature; and the fact that it is the genii of poets and not the poets themselves who are encountered gives opportunities for characterisation by physical description which are only occasionally, but then quite deftly, taken.

The second work in narrative form is the story of *Ḥayy ibn-Yaqẓān* by Ibn-Ṭufayl (d. 1185), which is considered as philosophy in a later section (p. 138). From the standpoint of literary history it may be noted that Ibn-Ṭufayl took over the exact title and the broad theme—the attainment of the highest Truth by the exercise of human faculties—of an earlier work by the Eastern philosopher Avicenna or Ibn-Sīnā (980–1037). But whereas Avicenna's work was a philosophical discourse and the hero's name—Alive, son of Awake—no more than an obvious symbol, Ibn-Ṭufayl combined it with a popular tale concerning a boy brought up by a gazelle, and gave flesh and blood to his speculations by depicting the mental development of an island recluse unencumbered with traditional beliefs and untrammelled with social bonds—a forerunner of Rousseau's *Émile*. In it the unlikely marriage of philosophy with popular story-telling has given Arabic literature its most cogent and arresting narrative until modern times.

3. *The Religious Sciences and History*

For the various intellectual disciplines, as for poetry, the political disorder which followed the breakdown of the Umayyad caliphate was a period when what had been quietly growing burst into flower. That this should happen in these disciplines was no doubt due in large part to what had been done in the third quarter of the tenth century—in the later years of ʿAbd-ar-Raḥmān III and under al-Ḥakam II—in building up libraries and encouraging scholars from the heartlands to settle in Spain. The temper of the age must also have helped, for the self-awareness and self-confidence created under ʿAbd-ar-Raḥmān III seem to have persisted even long after the Umayyads had disappeared. It is therefore not surprising that in the eleventh and twelfth centuries Spain produced men of wide-embracing scholarship, of whom the greatest achieved fame in the heartlands, while at the disappearance of most of Islamic Spain in the thirteenth century scholars from al-Andalus were able to find employment in North Africa, Egypt and Syria.

Far and away the most outstanding scholar of al-Andalus in the eleventh century was Ibn-Ḥazm of Cordova (994–1064), whose name is sometimes europeanised as Abenhazam.[26] There is a curious point about his genealogy. He claimed that an ancestor of Persian descent had come to Spain as a client of a member of the Umayyad family; and certain later biographers accept this claim. Yet some of his contemporaries twitted him on being really of an indigenous Spanish family from west of Seville.[27] He certainly felt himself identified with the Arabs in general and the Umayyad family in particular, and was a bitter opponent of the Christians. One of his minor works was a treatise on Arab genealogies.

His father held various prominent posts under al-Manṣūr the ʿĀmirid and his son al-Muẓaffar (d. 1008), and doubtless continued to be immersed in the troubled affairs of al-Andalus between that date and his own death in 1012.

PLATE 14. Tile mosaic and stucco wall decoration in the Salón de los Embajadores, Alhambra.

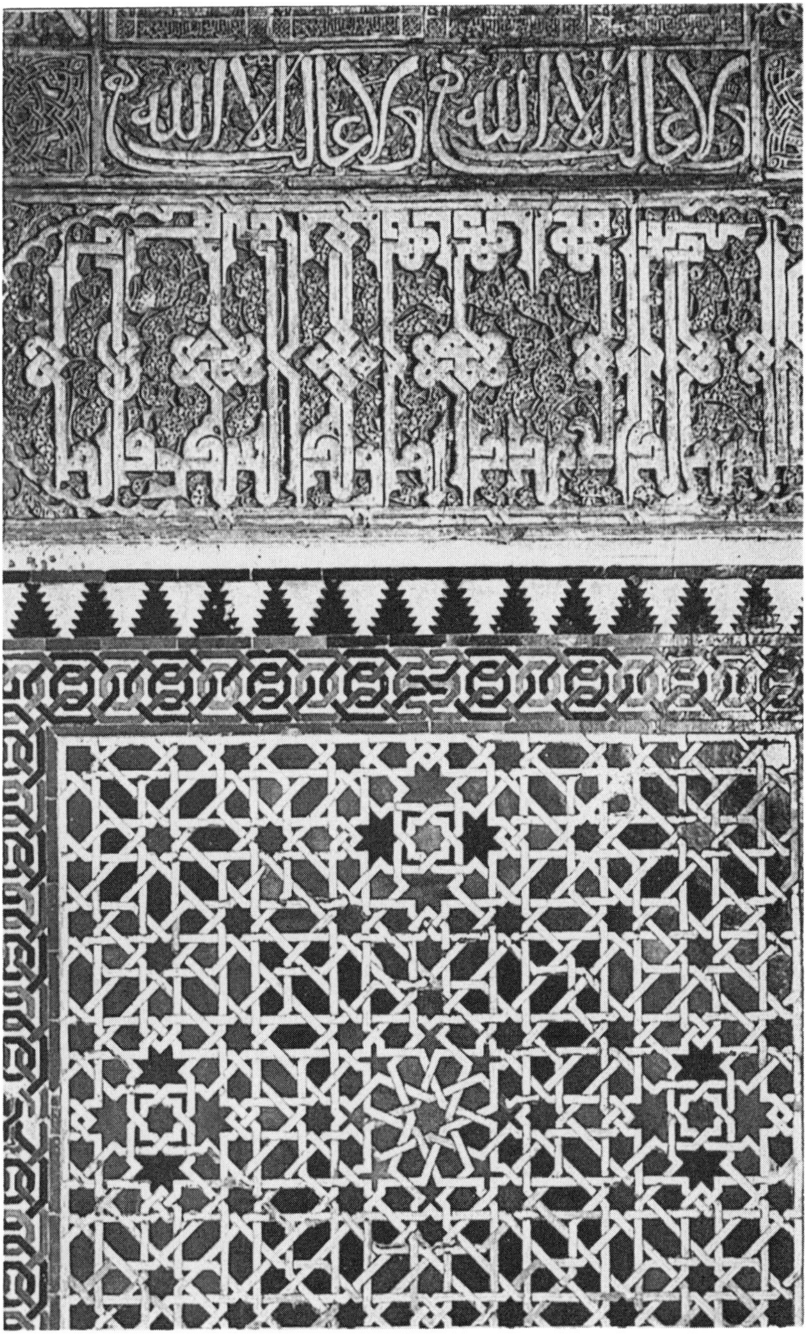

Ibn-Ḥazm's education must have been almost complete by this time, since the disintegration of the ruling institution began in 1009. There are scattered references to the family moving from one mansion or estate to another, until in 1013 they settled at Játiva near Valencia. By 1016 Ibn-Ḥazm seems to have been involved in politics as a supporter of the Umayyads, but his career as an administrator was very unsettled and included fighting and imprisonments. In December 1023 he became chief minister to one of the short-lived Umayyad caliphs, but seven weeks later the caliph had been assassinated and he himself once more thrown into prison. For a short time within the period 1027–31 he is reported to have held another political appointment, but before long he withdrew completely from politics and devoted himself entirely to scholarship.

His first prose work, *The Ring of the Dove*,[28] is a distinct surprise coming from one who subsequently attained high rank as a jurist and theologian, for it is about love and lovers with copious vivid anecdotes. While it expresses something of his own youthful experiences and interests, it is perhaps best understood as arising from his interest in the Arabic language and as exercising his skill in the use of it; the prose is carefully composed, and elegant verses of his own are inserted. This concern for language is a connecting link between *The Ring of the Dove* and the later theological system.

Ibn-Ḥazm's first instruction in the religious sciences had been derived from the Mālikism dominant in Spain, and was mainly limited to considering the details of the legal system in its practical application; but it was impossible to keep an acute student from asking questions about the justification of particular prescriptions, for in Spain there were now both Traditionists of great learning and

---

PLATE 15. Stucco wall decoration in the Patio de los Leones, Alhambra, Granada.

Shāfi'ite jurists, and the latter must have lectured about the "roots" or basic principles of the legal structure. Ibn-Ḥazm went deeply into the study of Traditions, and actually wrote a large book on law from the Shāfi'ite standpoint. By 1027, however, he was beginning to be dissatisfied with the Shāfi'ite system, and was coming under the influence of one of his earlier professors of literature who now introduced him to the Ẓāhirite school of jurisprudence, henceforward his spiritual home. Ẓāhirism was the creation of Dāwūd al-Iṣbahānī (d. 884), and made its central principle the retention of the "plain meaning" (*ẓāhir*) of the words of the Qur'ān and the Traditions. This central principle was relevant primarily to the attempt to harmonise apparently contradictory statements in the primary texts without falling into metaphorical interpretation (which was condemned in conservative circles).

The attraction of Ẓāhirism for Ibn-Ḥazm must have been great. Hitherto it had been merely a legal school or rite, but Ibn-Ḥazm now attempted on the same central principle to establish also a system of dogmatic theology. In this attempt there would seem to be evolving a combination of the fundamental Arab conception of language (and of the relation of language to knowledge) with a speculative tendency, which was probably of Iberian origin (since it may also be exemplified in the philosophical achievements of the following century). Language for the Muslim Arabs was no mere human convention but something created by God to be appropriate to the things to which it refers. The Qur'ān as the speech of God must be a perfect vehicle to convey to men what he wanted to convey. So the chief work of the scholar is to understand what God meant by the Qur'ān and, secondly, what is meant by the various sayings of Muḥammad. This understanding, however, presupposes wide familiarity with the Qur'ān and Traditions (including knowing the Qur'ān by heart), and the most scrupulous care by succeeding generations of scholars in transmitting accurately the precise verbal form of these scriptural texts. Such a conception was very general among Muslim scholars and by no means confined to the Ẓāhirites, but it was the Ẓāhirite Ibn-Ḥazm who took it most seriously and tried to work out its implications.

Ibn-Ḥazm seems to have had considerable influence on the later intellectual outlook of al-Andalus, but in theology he had no professed followers. Some of his pupils adopted Ẓāhirism in law, at least for a time, and the Ẓāhirite school continued for a century or two, though always with only a tiny body of adherents. Ibn-Ḥazm's tongue was proverbially sharp, and he made many enemies. For a time he found refuge in Majorca, but disputes there led to his expulsion. The closing years of his life were spent on the family estate near Niebla (west of Seville), and he died there in 1064.

Apart from his works on legal theory most attention has been given by recent scholars to his book on sects. It has been hailed as the first work ever on comparative religion, but this is not quite accurate. For one thing there are several earlier heresiologies in Arabic, and for another the aim was polemical and not descriptive. The intermingling of religions in Spain presumably drove a scholar like Ibn-Ḥazm to think out the position of his own religion over against its rivals. Altogether some three dozen works by Ibn-Ḥazm are still extant, though some indeed are little more than pamphlets, and they cover a wide range. In addition to those mentioned there is a work on ethics (which has been translated into Spanish), a critique (based, according to the biographers, on inadequate understanding) of Aristotelian logic, and an epistle defending al-Andalus against the charge of neglecting the biography of its intellectuals.[29]

Because Ibn-Ḥazm is outstanding he was not altogether typical. A first-rate scholar who became known in the heartlands but was more in accordance with the Andalusian ethos is Ibn-ʿAbd-al-Barr (978–1071).[30] Though he studied only in Cordova, he corresponded with scholars in the East (the heartlands) and became the greatest Traditionist of his time in Spain and North Africa. His studies and writings included various cognate disciplines such as Arab genealogy and the life and campaigns of Muḥammad. A collection of biographies of the Companions of Muḥammad—it was always a Companion who was first in the chain of transmission of a Tradition—attracted much attention and prepared the way for more complete collections.

His most original work, however, was one of which an abbreviated title would be, *The Exposition and Excellence of Knowledge*. In method this is a work typical of the Traditionist movement, for it consists almost exclusively of anecdotes about the sayings and doings of Muḥammad and various distinguished early Muslims, together with reports of the views held by scholars; he never gives his own views directly, though they may sometimes be inferred from such statements as that all jurists and scholars, with two exceptions, agree that analogical reasoning (*qiyās*) is permissible in legal decisions but not in theology. The choice of topics, however, is of great interest, and includes matters connected with the Arab conception of knowledge (as just described above), such as: the obligation to seek knowledge; the superiority of scholarship to piety and to martyrdom; whether it is desirable to write down knowledge (a procedure abhorrent to the oral culture of the pre-Islamic Arabs); travelling in quest of knowledge; the respect due from pupil to teacher; the attitude of scholars to rulers; the sources of legal and religious knowledge; and the types of argument possible in these fields. In this he shows a tendency to move away from the rigid Mālikism of the tenth century, and indeed explicitly condemns *taqlīd* or the blind following of authority. It is not surprising to learn that he first belonged to the Ẓāhirite school, and that, though he later adhered to the dominant Mālikite school—rising to be qāḍī of Lisbon—he was thought to have had

Shāfi'ite leanings. In the middle period of his long life he lived in various towns on or near the eastern seaboard, and his death also occurred there at Játiva.

Further light is thrown on the conditions in which scholars lived at this period by the life of al-Ḥumaydī. He was born in Majorca before 1029, his father having gone there from a suburb of Cordova, presumably because of the unsettled state of affairs. In Majorca al-Ḥumaydī came under the influence of Ibn-Ḥazm, and gained an excellent knowledge of Traditions and kindred subjects. He also studied under Ibn-'Abd-al-Barr, possibly in Cordova. In 1056 he set out on a study-journey to the East, which included making the pilgrimage to Mecca and spending some time in study there. He is also said to have learnt Traditions in Tunisia, Egypt, Damascus and Baghdad. Whether he returned to Spain for a time is not clear. He accepted the Ẓāhirite outlook of his teacher Ibn-Ḥazm, and suffered on account of the general opposition to this rite. It was because of this opposition that he eventually settled in Baghdad. Besides some competent but not noteworthy works on Traditions he was also prevailed on by friends in Baghdad to write an account of the learned men of Spain, and this he did from memory. He died in Baghdad in 1095, one of the first emigrants from Spain in an easterly direction.

The continuing high standards of scholarship in al-Andalus despite the troubles of the times are vouched for not merely by the names and biographies of several scholars during the next century and a half and by the lists of surviving manuscripts but above all by the fame attained in the heartlands by Qāḍī 'Iyāḍ (1083–1149). He is probably the chief figure of the Almoravid period. Born in Ceuta in the African part of the Almoravid empire, he studied in Cordova, but eventually returned to Ceuta as qāḍī. He was promoted to a similar post in Granada, but after a short time there moved on (in 1137) to Cordova. The troubled situation as the end of the Almoravid dominion approached was doubtless the reason for his withdrawal to Marrakesh, where he died in 1149.

He had the reputation of being the greatest Traditionist of the Islamic west in his day, and has left behind several books of average quality on jurisprudence and the study of Traditions, as well as a collection of biographies of Mālikite jurists. One work, however, known as the *Shifā'* ("cure"), raised him far above the average; there still exist more than twenty commentaries on it, written from the fourteenth to nineteenth centuries. Though the full title speaks of the "rights" of the Prophet, it is essentially a book in praise of him in which his figure is raised to supernatural stature. The existence of miracles performed by him is emphasised (in opposition to the theologians who insisted that his only miracle was the Qur'ān itself); his moral perfection is described; his preservation from error and blemish is asserted. The book thus marks a large step forward in the development of the theological doctrine of the person of Muḥammad, and it was presumably for this reason that it attracted so many commentators. It is tempting to connect the general attitude of the book with the saint-worship prevalent in North Africa. Though 'Iyāḍ's grandfather is said to have emigrated from al-Andalus first to Fez and then to Ceuta, the family may well have been originally Berber and almost certainly had North African blood on the female side. Thus heredity probably combined with environment to foster the outlook characteristic of North Africa.[31]

The Mālikism of the Almoravid period was thus changing from that of the late tenth century, and Mālikite scholars were including in their scope much more than practical legal details. As the threat from the Almohads began to appear in North Africa (from about 1125 onwards), the Mālikites supporting the Almoravids felt impelled to attack not merely the teaching of Ibn-Tūmart and his Almohad followers but also the Ash'arite theology now dominant in Baghdad which was thought (not altogether correctly) to have been the major influence in the formation of his views. There were particularly vicious attacks on the distinguished Ashʿarite theologian and mystic, al-Ghazālī; books were written criticising him, his views were officially condemned as heretical, and his great work, *The Revival of the Religious Sciences*, was publicly burned (apparently on the order of the Qāḍī ʿIyāḍ).

With the establishment of Almohad power in Spain from 1145 onwards, the Mālikite jurists ceased to have the official support they had enjoyed under the Almoravids, but some at least retained their appointments. As time went on the Almohad rulers found they could not do without the Mālikites and the section of the population whose mouthpiece they were. Though the Almohads started off with an official theology, this was not necessarily connected with any one system of jurisprudence. Abū-Yūsuf Yaʿqūb, who ruled from 1184 to 1199, is said to have favoured the Ẓāhirites. The most illustrious jurist of the time supporting the régime was Ibn-Rushd (1126–98), who, because he became one of the world's great philosophers, is seldom thought of as a jurist. Yet he came of a family of jurists, himself rose to being qāḍī of Seville and then of Cordova, and in 1188 seems to have completed an important work on jurisprudence, apparently written for the most part twenty years earlier. The book deals with the "differences" between the various legal rites (or schools), and pays special attention to the types of argument used by each to justify its particular decisions.[32] This subject of the "roots" of law was one originally avoided by the Mālikites of Spain, but cultivated by the smaller groups of Ẓāhirites and Shāfiʿites, and it seems likely that it was these groups who were the chief supporters of the Almohads in jurisprudence.

Finally, historical writing in Spain may be mentioned

briefly.[33] It is not inappropriate in this chapter, since many of the historical and biographical writers were also jurists. The most important of the earlier historians, in the view of Lévi-Provençal, is Ibn-Ḥayyān (d. 1076), whose work, though surviving only in parts, contains much valuable and reliable information. A contemporary, Ṣā'id, qāḍī of Toledo (d. 1070), left a compendium of universal history (translated into French in 1935 as *Livre des catégories des nations*) which divides the peoples into those which cultivated science and those which did not, and indicates the extent of Muslim knowledge of non-Muslim cultures at this period. Many collections of biographical notices were also produced in al-Andalus, mostly of local scholars. Practically all this historical writing is of more concern to modern scholars for its content than as a literary production.

There is a sense in which the culture of Islamic Spain was continued in North Africa, and it is therefore fitting to conclude by mentioning the name of Ibn-Khaldūn (1332–1406) who, though born in Tunis, belonged to an Arab family which had lived in Spain since the eighth century and had latterly played an important part in the life of Seville until shortly before the capture of that city by the Christians. He is the author of an extensive historical work whose later volumes deal in detail with the history of the various dynasties of North Africa. He has attracted much attention, however, by the *Introduction* or *Muqaddima* to this history which is generally regarded as a pioneer work in sociology. Though he lived mostly in various parts of North Africa, including Egypt, and only spent a little over two years in Spain at Granada (1362–5), his most recent translator has judged that "his basic loyalty to Spain and its civilisation" was a deep influence underlying his work.[34] He thus illustrates one of the channels through which al-Andalus made contributions to the Islamic world as a whole.

4. *Philosophy and Mysticism*

It has been noted above (p. 67) that philosophy was cultivated in al-Andalus in the early tenth century by Ibn-Masarra and his school. Though there are traces of a continuing interest in philosophical ideas, no scholar of note can be described as a philosopher until we come to Avempace, also known as Ibn-Bājja (d. 1138). He was born at Saragossa, but later lived for some years at Seville and Granada. Towards the end of his life he moved to the Almoravid capital at Fez, where he was apparently poisoned by a distinguished physician. His chief work was called *The Rule of the Solitary*, and in general may be said to express a moral protest against the materialism and worldliness of the ruling classes of the day. Because society is so corrupt, he maintained, the man who has seen its true condition must keep himself detached from it, at least in thought. There is genuine ethical passion behind this work of Avempace, but one is bound to remember that the conservative Mālikite jurists were in control of intellectual life under the Almoravids, and that little else than retirement and solitude was open to Avempace. For the pure philosopher as distinct from the historian the great interest of his work is in his analysis of the "spiritual forms" or ideas present in human thought.[35]

The seed sown by Avempace bore wonderful fruit after the fall of the Almoravids and the establishment of Almohad rule in al-Andalus. Reasons can be discerned for the possibility of great philosophical achievements under the Almohads. The founder of the Almohad movement, Ibn-Tūmart (*c.* 1080–1130), had been a theologian and not a philosopher, but he had favoured the more philosophical forms of theology. It is almost certain that he had not been a pupil of al-Ghazālī himself (d. 1111),[36] the great theologian who had mastered the Neoplatonic philosophy of the day and, while criticising it vigorously, had shown that much of it was compatible with sound theological doctrine; but he had been in touch with this line of thought. Moreover the intellectual defence of Mālikism under the Almoravids (as has been seen) had included attacks on al-Ghazālī as well as on Almohad theology. Thus once the intellectual opposition came into power there was likely to be a climate of opinion favourable to philosophy; and this indeed happened.

The first important philosopher under the Almohads was Ibn-Ṭufayl (*c.* 1105–85), also known in medieval times as Abubacer from his "father-name" (*kunya*) of Abū-Bakr. He was born at Guadix near Granada, and after being secretary to the local governor rose to the position of vizier and court-physician to the Almohad ruler Abū-Yaʿqūb Yūsuf (1163–84). His philosophy was given to the world in a partly allegorical form (perhaps to parry opposition) in the romance of *Ḥayy ibn-Yaqẓān* ("Alive son of Awake"), which has been translated into various European languages.[37]

The hero of the romance, Ḥayy, grows up from babyhood on a deserted island without human contact, suckled and nurtured by a gazelle. By his own reflections on what he sees around him he gradually works out a complete philosophical system, including a doctrine of God, and attains some measure of mystical ecstasy. Another young man Asāl now comes to the island seeking withdrawal from the world in order to engage in mystical contemplation (in the tradition of Avempace). When the two meet and compare notes, they find that the philosophical religion of Ḥayy is identical with the position of Asāl, reached by philosophical criticism of traditional religion. Ḥayy is now filled with enthusiasm for converting the common people on the inhabited island to his philosophical religion, but when the two set out and attempt this they find that the people do not want what they have to give and will not accept it.

This story, which is told with great charm, clearly refers in the first place to the contemporary problems of the relation between philosophy and religion. Ḥayy may be said to stand for pure philosophy, and Asāl for philosophical theology, perhaps such as that of Ibn-Tūmart. The ruler of the inhabited island is Salāmān, who is said to favour the literal meaning of texts (*ẓāhir*) and to be averse to metaphorical interpretation (*ta'wīl*), and may therefore stand for the Ẓāhirites and other jurists supporting the Almohads (but perhaps not for the Mālikites). Ibn-Ṭufayl's solution of his problems is thus a negative one. The philosophical religion is true but it cannot be used directly to guide the affairs of state or the lives of the ordinary people. A few privileged individuals may through philosophy fulfil the highest potentialities of human life, but they only do so through withdrawal from the active life of the world. One is reminded of the philosopher-kings of Plato's *Republic*, who found their true life in the contemplation of the Good in itself. What Ibn-Ṭufayl does not explain is how the contemplation or mystical ecstasy of the philosophers is able to contribute to the well-being of the worldly state consisting of ordinary people.

The other great philosopher of the Almohad period—in some ways the greatest philosopher of all who wrote in Arabic—is Averroes or Ibn-Rushd (1126–98), who has already been mentioned as a jurist. He was a friend of Ibn-Ṭufayl, whom for a short time (about 1183) he followed as physician at the Almohad court. He had originally been introduced by Ibn-Ṭufayl, probably about 1153, to the Almohad prince and future ruler Abū-Ya'qūb Yūsuf. Though the young Averroes was already well-versed in the Greek sciences, he was afraid and denied his knowledge of such matters when the prince asked him whether the philosophers thought the heavens eternal or created. It was only when the prince turned to Ibn-Ṭufayl and spoke freely of Plato, Aristotle and others, that he ventured to join in the conversation. Despite this inauspicious beginning he formed a close friendship with the prince. The latter's son and successor, Abū-Yūsuf Yaʿqūb al-Manṣūr, was also friendly with the philosopher, but about 1195, to gain the support of the Mālikite jurists in the campaign against the Castilians, had to remove Averroes from his post as qāḍī of Cordova and order his books to be burnt; soon afterwards, however, he made up for this by installing him in the court at Marrakesh.

The most important philosophical work of Averroes is contained in the commentaries he wrote on many of the writings of Aristotle. He had penetrated deeply into the thought of Aristotle, and for this reason was able to interpret his writings in a genuinely Aristotelian fashion. Previously the Muslim thinkers' understanding of Aristotle had been largely dependent on the Neoplatonic tradition which distorted his teaching in various ways, and minimised the difference between him and Plato. Much confusion had been caused by the circulation of an Arabic version of a Neoplatonic book under the title of *The Theology of Aristotle*. One of the great merits of Averroes was thus to recover the true Aristotle and to transmit his thought to Europe. This came about when Christian and Jewish scholars in Spain translated the commentaries of Averroes into Latin or Hebrew. This introduction of Aristotle to Europe was one of the chief factors contributing to the great achievement of Thomism, though Averroes is not to be blamed because his view of the relation of reason and revelation was distorted by the so-called Latin Averroists into the theory of the "double truth".

Although under the Almoravids the Mālikites had combined an attack on al-Ghazālī with that on the Almohads, Averroes felt constrained to defend philosophy against the criticisms made by al-Ghazālī in his book *The Inconsistency of the Philosophers* (written about 1095). In his defence and reply, *The Inconsistency of the Inconsistency*, Averroes examined the earlier work paragraph by paragraph, refuted in detail its strictures on the philosophers, and incidentally expounded his own belief in the ability of reason to comprehend the ultimate secrets of the universe.[38] This book was of the highest quality and had some influence on European thought (a Latin translation having been made by 1328); but it was too late and too much on the periphery to bring about any revival of philosophy in the heartlands of Islam. In so far as philosophy was now cultivated there, it was by theologians, especially of the Ashʿarite school; and their philosophy was subordinate to theological dogma. Though the work of Averroes was known in the east, its outlook was so foreign to these men that it had nothing to say to them.

Apart from his purer Aristotelianism Averroes differs from Ibn-Ṭufayl in his more positive attitude in respect of the relation of philosophy to religion. Averroes was deeply convinced that both philosophy and religion are true; this was the basis of his own life in which he combined philosophical writing with the work of a qāḍī. In a short essay, now translated into English under the title *The Harmony of Religion and Philosophy*, he insists that, since philosophy is true and the revealed scriptures are true, there cannot be any disharmony between them. He then shows in some detail how apparent contradictions are to be reconciled. Though philosophers may occasionally be mistaken in points of detail, philosophy is in general sound; and therefore the reconciliation has to be effected by finding interpretations of scriptural statements which are in harmony with accepted philosophical doctrine.

From this standpoint Averroes justifies the participation of the philosopher in the active life of the day. The religious ideas of the ordinary people are valid when properly understood and interpreted; and therefore the philosopher does not avoid contact with popular religion, but "should choose the best religion of his period", accept its formulations and explain them. In so doing he is contributing to the life of the state, in which religion has an important function. So fully aware is Averroes of the place of religion in society, that he considers a revealed religion—when philosophically understood, of course—superior to the religion of pure reason. Perhaps the difference between Ibn-Ṭufayl and Averroes on this point is due to the moulding of the thought of the first by Almoravid and Mālikite hostility to philosophy, in contrast to the toleration and friendship generally experienced by philosophers under the Almohads.

With Averroes, philosophy reached its highwater mark in Islamic Spain. The period of toleration was over by the time of his death, for the serious political situation had brought the Mālikites back into power. There is sometimes talk of the "philosophy" of Muḥyī-d-Dīn ibn-al-ʿArabī, but it is rather a theosophy. A somewhat younger man—probably born a few years before 1200—but with a greater claim to be a philosopher is Ibn-Sabʿīn (d. 1270). He was born and brought up in Spain and belonged to the Spanish tradition, but soon preferred to go to North Africa, and ended his life in Mecca by opening his veins, it is said. A book of some interest has been ascribed to him (though doubtfully), known as *Answers to Sicilian Questions*; these were questions asked of the Muslim scholars in Ceuta by the emperor Frederick II (by the intermediary of the Almohad ruler of the time). The philosophy was less Aristotelian and more Neoplatonic than that of Averroes. This is not surprising since Ibn-Sabʿīn was also a mystic.[39]

It is difficult to write explicitly about ṣūfism or mysticism in Spain, partly because it is intertwined with the philosophy studied in Spain, and partly because it is dependent on the development of mysticism in North Africa and elsewhere. The connection of mysticism with philosophy goes back to Ibn-Masarra (p. 67 above). The names of some of his disciples are known who were active in the later tenth and early eleventh centuries; but the distinctive Masarrite movement came to an end when one man put himself forward as a wonder-working leader and became immersed in politics. The Masarrite mystics had had a centre in Pechina as well as that in the capital, Cordova; and in the neighbouring Almeria another mystical movement is found in the second half of the eleventh century. This movement was given definite form by Ibn-al-ʿIrrīf (d. 1141), and had secondary centres at Seville, Granada and in Algarve (Portugal). The Almoravid rulers apparently became suspicious of the possible political implications of the movement as their hold on al-Andalus weakened, and summoned both Ibn-al-ʿIrrīf and his supporter in Seville, Ibn-Barrajān, to North Africa, where both died. The leader in Algarve managed to maintain himself in political independence from 1141 to 1151.[40]

According to the most distinguished student of the mysticism of Islamic Spain, Miguel Asín Palacios, the influence of Masarrite ideas is also to be seen in the greatest of the mystics of al-Andalus, Muḥyī-d-Dīn ibn-al-ʿArabī (1165–1240).[41] He was born in Murcia, and studied both in Spain and North Africa, at this time united under the Almohads. It was probably in Seville that he came under the influence of Ibn-al-ʿIrrīf and Ibn-Barrajān. In 1201, however, he went east on pilgrimage, and spent the rest of his life in such places as Mecca, Baghdad and Damascus, thereby coming into touch with the various strands of mysticism in the heartlands, including the Ḥanbalite. His literary production was vast, and took up into itself much of the material found in earlier mystical writers. Asín Palacios also asserts Christian influences, though other scholars tend to minimise these. Ibn-al-ʿArabī makes much of the conception of the Logos, which he identifies with Muḥammad or the reality of Muḥammad; but this is not parallel to the Christian doctrine of the Logos, for Ibn-al-ʿArabī's system in general is pantheistic and monistic. To go into such matters in detail, however, belongs rather to the general study of Islamic mysticism.

Finally it is to be noticed that men born in al-Andalus made important contributions to the growth of the dervish or mystical order of the Shādhiliyya. Abū-Madyan of Tlemcen (d. 1193), sometimes regarded as co-founder of the order along with ash-Shādhilī (d. 1258), came originally from Spain, as did also the latter's chief disciple and successor, Abū-'l-'Abbās al-Mursī, the man from Murcia (d. 1287). The most important of these Andalusians who spent their maturity in North Africa was Ibn-'Abbād of Ronda (1333–90), who spent much of his life in Rabat and was latterly in Fez.[42] He is chiefly remembered for a commentary on one of the basic works of the order and for a collection of "letters of spiritual direction".

5. *The Art of the Eleventh and Twelfth Centuries*

The art of Islamic Spain under the "party kings", the Almoravids and the Almohads is worthy of the attention of the historian in that it both throws light on some of the general questions he is trying to answer and also introduces further complexities. One of the complexities is that the course of development in the visual arts differs considerably from that in literature. The reason may be that the two forms proceed mainly from two distinct social milieus. Works of art, especially of architecture, were commissioned by the ruling élite in any given period, and were executed, for the most part, by members of the body of craftsmen who had inherited the necessary skills.

The most notable remaining architectural work of the period of "party kings" is the Aljaféria of Saragossa, a

PLATE 16. Pool of the Partal and the Torre de las Damas in the Alhambra.

palace built by the local ruler Abū-Ja'far al-Muqtadir (1049–81). As compared with works of the tenth century it shows an increasing interest in decoration. Arches are elaborately lobed, and the interlacing geometrical designs become more subtle. There is a certain love of contrast apparent in the alternation of plain areas and panels filled with elaborate decoration. All this is in a natural line of development from the art of the Umayyad period.

In Spain itself there are no outstanding works of the Almoravid period, but the general character of their art can be discerned from various buildings in North Africa now that—comparatively recently—the plaster with which they were covered in the Almohad period has been removed. The Almoravids made use of craftsmen from al-Andalus, so that the style of the architecture of Islamic Spain was transferred to the southern shore of the Mediterranean. The tendency to cover an area entirely with ornamentation is specially noticeable in many examples of Almoravid work. On the other hand, the religious beliefs of the Almoravids, and their supporters the Mālikite jurists, do not seem in any way to have affected their artistic productions.

With the Almohads, on the contrary, the element of puritanism in their religious outlook led to a reaction against the luxuriant decoration of the immediately preceding period. It was for this reason that some of the Almoravid work was plastered over. The greater simplicity of Almohad art is immediately apparent especially in the North African examples, where it also is felt to have an air of grandeur. This is not so evident in Almohad works in Spain itself. One of the chief Almohad monuments, the Giralda of Seville (now the bell-tower of the cathedral and illustrated in Plate 9) is closer to earlier

PLATE 17. The intersecting binding arches of a Dome at the Mosque, Cordova; a style which influenced later Italian Renaissance architecture.

Spanish styles than to the contemporary style of North Africa.

Among the points of wider import to be noticed there is the ready acceptance by the new Berber rulers of the architectural tradition of al-Andalus. Because their previous material culture was of the simplest, they had really no alternative to taking over the tradition and no way even of contributing to it. The theological ideas underlying the Almoravid and Almohad movements, though emphasising the distinctively Islamic moment (and the superiority of Islam to Christianity), had little direct influence on artistic productions. Because the tradition of al-Andalus was definitely Islamic and anti-Christian, the Muslim zealots had no qualms about taking it over. They may indeed have felt that there was something specifically Islamic about its geometrical and stylised floral ornamentation.

(10)

THE LAST OF ISLAMIC SPAIN

1. *The Naṣrids of Granada*

THE founder of the Naṣrid dynasty, as already noted (p. 111), was Muḥammad ibn-Yūsuf ibn-Naṣr, also known as Ibn-al-Aḥmar. Though it was originally at Jaen that he set himself up as a ruler (about 1231), the progress of the Reconquista under Ferdinand III of Castile, and in particular the loss of Jaen itself in 1245, forced him to retire southwards and to make Granada, which he had occupied in 1235, the seat of his government. When it became clear to him that he could not indefinitely keep the forces of Castile at bay with his slender military resources, he decided to become a vassal of Ferdinand, as several other local Muslim rulers were doing. In this capacity he gave support to his liege-lord in the campaigns which led to the capture of Seville and the lower valley of the Guadalquivir, and in other subsequent campaigns against Muslims. The state which was thus created extended from Tarifa (just beyond Gibraltar) in the west to some twenty or thirty miles beyond Almeria in the east—in all about 240 miles. In the north the frontier was probably nearer to Jaen than to Granada, at a distance of sixty or seventy miles from the sea as the crow flies.

When Muḥammad I of Granada became the vassal of Castile, he was not the only Muslim ruler in this position. The others, however, gradually disappeared and were replaced by Christian governors, the last to go being the emir of Murcia in 1264. It is therefore worth asking why the kingdom of Granada should have managed to keep its independence for two centuries and a half. Various reasons may be suggested, though no single one of them seems to be decisive. Muḥammad I appears to have been a good vassal to Ferdinand and his son, and thereby to have merited generous treatment; and by the time of his death in 1273 the acceptance of an independent Granada may have been a fixed point in the policy of Castile. Castile, too, with many Muslim subjects, may have felt that it was useful to have a Muslim state near to which the more discontented could flee for refuge. Perhaps, however, the main emphasis should be laid on two geographical factors—the mountainous nature of the country, and the nearness to Africa. Most of the territory of Granada consisted of relatively high mountains, and this natural defence was reinforced by strong fortresses and fortress towns (like Ronda) at the points where attack was easiest. So long as things went well, the rulers of Castile probably felt that no attempt to advance their frontiers was worth the military cost. Moreover the nearness of Africa made it possible for the Naṣrids to appeal for help from time to time to the new Muslim rulers of Morocco, the Marīnid dynasty. This meant that they were never completely at the mercy of Castile, even though they were careful to give the Marīnids no opportunity of adding Granada to their African domains.

The state of Granada was very consciously Islamic. A welcome was given to refugees from the rest of Spain. Arabic was the only language used. Though there were Jews in the state, there were no Mozarabic Christians; but it is not clear whether this was because of some definite enactment, or because the attitude of ordinary Muslims made life too unpleasant for them. This emphasis on Islam and on the defence of Islam is understandable after the concern for the holy war shown by the Almoravids and the

Almohads and after the growing self-consciousness of the Christian Reconquista during the period of success from 1212 to 1248.

On many aspects of the history of the Naṣrid state little information is available. Most is known about its relations to the Christian states, since there is material about this in their chronicles. The period of greatest brilliance was from 1344 to 1396, during which time the finest parts of the Alhambra were built. On the whole the state was very prosperous, through its intensive agriculture, its urban handicrafts and its trade. There were many internal difficulties, however. Quarrels about the succession among members of the ruling family, each with supporting interests, were frequent, especially from the last decade of the fourteenth century. The consciously Islamic attitude of the state favoured an increase in the power of the jurists; and they, together with the African mercenaries and certain urban elements, tended to favour war. Opposed to them were the ruling élite, the merchants and the peasants, whose interests were much better served by peace.

The end of the Naṣrid realm came about as much through its own internal weaknesses as through the growing strength of the Christians. This strength was very much increased by the union of Aragon and Castile through the marriage of Ferdinand and Isabella, Isabella ascending the throne of Castile in 1474 and Ferdinand (II) that of Aragon in 1479. Even before this, however, the capture of Gibraltar in 1462 showed that the Christian powers were again on the move. Yet the final debacle might have been postponed had the Muslim leaders not lost their nerve and given way to impatience. In 1481, before the end of a period of truce, some of them seized the castle of Zahara from the Christians, and this provocative pinprick doubtless led Ferdinand and Isabella to the resolve to make an end of Granada. An out-and-out military attack was avoided. Instead Ferdinand availed himself of the

Muslims' divisions, and kept one party of them at peace by supporting them while his armies were launched against the other party in isolation. In this way he managed to capture Ronda (1485) and Malaga (1487) in the west, and then Almeria (1489) in the east. The final campaign against Granada was launched in 1491, and before the end of the year the defenders had recognised the hopelessness of their position and agreed to surrender. Honourable terms were granted, and the surrender became effective in the first days of 1492. Romance has played round the scene when from a vantage-point on the hillside the last of the Naṣrids—the last Muslim ruler in Spain—Abū-ʿAbd-Allāh or Boabdil, bade farewell to al-Andalus.

2. *The Muslims under Christian Rule*

From one point of view the fall of the Naṣrids was the end of Islamic Spain; and yet from another point of view it was far from the end. To the historian of Islamic culture what was happening in some non-Muslim parts of Spain in the thirteenth and fourteenth centuries is at least as important as what was happening in Naṣrid Granada. To complete the story of Islamic Spain, then, it is necessary to look at the life and achievements of the Muslims who remained in Christian states.

Scholars' familiarity with the reputation of Christian Spain for intolerance, together with the prominence given to the idea of Reconquest, has sometimes suggested that, once a province came under Christian rule, there ceased to be any Muslims in it. Although Castile in particular favoured the policy of settling Christian colonists in unoccupied lands, it was far from the case that there were no Muslims under Christian rule. When Toledo was captured in 1085, many craftsmen remained; with them were also some scholars, and these played an important part in the transmission of Islamic science and philosophy to Europe.

After 1248 there were many Muslims in the Christian kingdoms. In the new Andalusian province of Castile they constituted a majority of the population, while in Aragon proper and the province of Valencia the Christians were a comparatively small minority. This state of affairs was inevitable; the rulers had to retain the Muslims because they were an essential part of the economy of the country, while for the Muslims there was no other region where they could exercise their skills adequately.

Those Muslims who continued in their former homes after the change of rule are known as Mudejars (Spanish, *mudéjares*), the word being derived from the Arabic *mudajjan*, "permitted to remain", with a suggestion of "tamed, domesticated". They had a position similar to that of the protected minorities in the Islamic states. They followed their own religion, laws and customs, and were free to carry on their crafts and to trade. Each local community had a Muslim head appointed by the king. In return for their privileges they paid a poll-tax or tribute. They constituted distinct communities, sometimes forced to mark themselves off by dress, and inhabited special quarters in the chief towns. Many were hard-working peasants in the country districts. Certain crafts were almost entirely in the hands of Mudejars.

The presence of the Mudejars in Christian Spain produced little in the way of the "historical events" on which nineteenth-century historians tended to concentrate. Yet their uneventful life is an indication of an important historical phenomenon—the existence of an economic structure and a material culture common to Christian and Muslim. In the Mudejar age—the thirteenth and fourteenth centuries—this economic structure and material culture reached out to embrace even those parts of northern Spain which had had practically no direct contact with Muslims. The most important pieces of evidence for this are artistic productions of the period.

At the same time it must be realised that there was selectivity in the assimilation of this culture by the Christians. What was clearly at variance with basic Christian conceptions was never taken over; and this applied to the higher levels of the intellectual life, particularly in the case of the ordinary Spanish Christian. Christian scholars from outside Spain, indeed, came to make contact with the living tradition of Greek philosophy in its Islamic dress, and much ink had to be spilt in separating what could from what could not be Christianised; but that does not belong specifically to the history of Spain.

By the beginning of the fifteenth century a change of attitude can be detected among the Spanish Christians. In part it may be due to economic grievances, for many of the Mudejars were wealthy. Certainly anti-Muslim prejudice began to appear among the common people. With the union of Spain under Ferdinand and Isabella such prejudice came to have some influence on policy. The old policy of religious tolerance still governed the terms of surrender granted to the inhabitants of Granada in 1492, but in the same year an edict was promulgated forcing the Jews throughout Spain to be baptised or to leave the country. Earlier, in 1478, the Inquisition had been "nationalised" in that the inquisitors for Spain were to be appointed by the king and queen and not by the Pope. This appears to have had the result that what was promoted, or even enforced, was not Christian orthodoxy *simpliciter*, but Christian orthodoxy as conceived by leading Spaniards.

Another facet of the new policy was seen in 1499 when the powerful Cardinal Ximénez de Cisneros visited Granada and had discussions with the jurists there. This was followed by the burning of specifically Islamic books and by forced conversions. The result was an insurrection which began in the following year and lasted into the one after that. By way of punishment the Muslims of Granada in 1502 were given the choice of baptism or exile. Many chose baptism, though without any change of basic conviction. In 1525 and 1526 similar measures were taken against Muslims in other provinces. Thereafter there were officially no Muslims in Spain, but for nearly a century the rulers of Spain had to cope with the problem of the Moriscos.

Various reasons can be given for this growth of intolerance in Spain after the long tradition of tolerance. There had been a time when it had been hoped that members of the three faiths could be welded into a unity; but it was becoming clear that this was not possible. Political unity under Ferdinand and Isabella, with its new potentialities for disunity, made a unity of spirit all the more necessary. The intransigence and defensive attitude of Granada in its closing decades doubtless contributed to the resolve of Ferdinand and Isabella to work for a genuine unity of outlook. By 1525 Spain, now growing into an imperial power, was aware of the Islamic threat to Europe by the Turkish advance towards Vienna (which was actually besieged in 1529). Commitments there and across the Atlantic were making the utmost demands on Spanish man-power; so that common-sense suggested the removal of potentially hostile elements from the base while so many of the reliable men of fighting age were out of the country.

There is said to have been some understanding that the Muslims were to be allowed forty years to carry out the measures of 1525 and 1526. Whether this is so or not, there was a revival of anti-Muslim legislation in 1566. The previous measures had not been effective. For one thing, Islamic religious practice in the heartlands and elsewhere had often permitted and justified *taqiyya* or the concealing of one's true religious beliefs where to reveal them would endanger one's life; and the Moriscos had apparently got official legal opinions from Muslim jurists outside Spain to the effect that in the circumstances of sixteenth-century

Spain such concealment of their attachment to Islam was permissible. Manuscripts are preserved known as *aljamiados*, which are written in the Spanish language but in Arabic characters; these contain expositions of Islamic faith and practice by and for Moriscos. An additional reason for intolerance was the factor, now making itself felt, of the relatively higher birth-rate among the Muslims, which was raising the proportion of Muslims in the population. On the other hand, the Moriscos' essential contributions to the economic and material life of Spain led many nobles in Aragon and Valencia to support them.

From 1566, then, the pressure on the Moriscos increased. Some of them revolted in 1569 and received help from the Ottoman governor of Algiers. Yet, despite the pressure, their communities remained largely intact in the towns owing to the self-contained character of their lives. They were thus proving an unassimilable element in the population. Finally between 1609 and 1614 came edicts of expulsion, as a result of which about half a million are said to have gone to North Africa. What happened in some places there throws interesting light on conditions in Spain. Though now among fellow-Muslims, some Moriscos showed themselves just as unassimilable as they had been in Christian Spain. Their culture was that common material culture of Spain, Islamic and Christian. In the Islamic atmosphere of North Africa, they became more than ever aware of their Spanishness and of their superiority to African Muslims, Berbers or others. Indeed something of Islamic Spain is preserved in certain cities of North Africa until the present day, so that Islamic Spain to this limited extent is still alive.

3. *Literature in a Period of Retreat*

This period in the literary history of Andalusia has been characterised, not unjustly, as a mere epilogue. There was no great inventive impulse, no startling poetic innovation. Rather was it—as indeed it was in the Islamic East also—an age of compilation and wide erudition, when the scholarship accumulated by succeeding generations was recorded or given final expression, often by expatriate Andalusians.

One such expatriate was the grammarian Ibn-Mālik (1208–74) who expounded the whole of Arabic grammar in two *urjūzas* of which the shorter, running to somewhat less than a thousand lines of doggerel verse,[1] is used to this day as a teaching text. Another who taught in the East was Abū-Ḥayyān (1257–1344), celebrated primarily as a grammarian but also well versed in a number of Islamic sciences; it is a measure of his erudition that he was the author of an important Turkish grammar, and is said also to have written an Ethiopic one. Yet another was Ibn-Sa'īd al-Maghribī (d. 1274), a man of many parts who compiled a much-prized anthology to which he contributed not a few verses of his own.

Those who remained within the shrinking Muslim domains in Spain were also living on accumulated capital, but the capital was large enough to enable them to live with dignity and elegance. Under the rule of the Naṣrids of Granada, and especially at court, in that Alhambra whose exquisitely carved palaces and pavilions rest lightly on slender pillars as deceptively frail-looking as a ballerina on her points, poets and prose-writers more conscious of their heritage than of approaching doom could yet display some of the sparkle of an earlier age.

Towering above all other literary figures of the time was that of Lisān-ad-Dīn ibn-al-Khaṭīb (1313–74). Several times vizier, chronicler, author of a useful biographical dictionary, he was also a master of ornamental prose who wrote numerous *maqāmas*, and a highly accomplished poet who composed both traditional odes and fine *muwashshaḥs*. He also composed an *urjūza* entitled *Raqm al-Ḥulal fi Naẓm ad-Duwal* recounting the history of Islam in the West, which one modern Arab considers worthy of the title of an Arab Shāh-Nāmeh,[2] though it never struck root in the imagination of the people as did the Persian epic. On the whole, he was notable not for the blazing of new trails but for his delicate workmanship, easy lilt, charming sentiment and felicitous imagery, as he sang of lovers trysting in idyllic surroundings, watched only by envious narcissi or by lilies that prick up their ears at their passing, sharing a destiny "faultless, except that it spent itself in the twinkling of an eye".

It was his protégé and successor Ibn-Zamrak (1333–93), the last of the great Andalusian poets, whose verses were used in decorating the walls of the Alhambra.

The Moriscos who found themselves under Christian rule had of course vastly different preoccupations. Not for them a literature of refinement dependent on the patronage of the great. Instead, they circulated among themselves works designed to counter the pressures to which their faith was subjected: expositions of canonical law; polemical tracts; some poetry in praise of the Prophet and on other Islamic themes; and not a few tales and legends derived from universal folklore, or inspired by ascetics, or growing out of Qur'ānic references to Moses and Joseph and Solomon and Alexander, or magnifying the deeds of Muḥammad and other Muslim heroes. This *aljamiado* literature, worded in Spanish although written in Arabic characters, can command no more than a passing reference in this survey; it is worth noting, however, that many popular tales were thus recorded which in a classical-minded Arabic-speaking society might have escaped the attention of the literate.

The profusion of popular narratives thus revealed is not without relevance to a consideration of the influences exerted by Andalusian literature outside Islamic Spain, influences by no means restricted to the period surveyed in this section, but which the Reconquista hastened and swelled.

On the one hand, the Islamic East had always had the opportunity of savouring the finest literary productions of al-Andalus, and to it the vogue of the *muwashshaḥ* had spread. Now, as the Muslim hold on the Peninsula was reduced and loosened, more and more of the leading families of al-Andalus and of her scholars sought the protection of fellow Muslims and the patronage of Muslim princes elsewhere, especially in North Africa. Tunis and then Fez became repositories of Andalusian culture, so that it is to a North African who studied in Fez, al-Maqqarī (d. 1631) that we owe a very great deal of the information we now have on al-Andalus and its literature.

On the other hand, Christians were bringing under their sway a mixed population with a culture some aspects of which they came to appreciate and assimilate into their own.

Already when the fortunes of the Muslims were in the ascendant, their learning had attracted scholars of all faiths. Spanish Jews in particular were directly indebted to Arab thought, and many of them—including the great Maimonides (1135–1204)—sat at the feet of Arabic-speaking teachers and wrote their books in Arabic. Even in belles-lettres, Hebrew poets—such as Ibn-Gabirol (1021–52)—were influenced by Arab prosody, and Hebrew *muwashshaḥs* were written which not only adopted the conventions of the Arabic form but were "in the overwhelming majority of cases . . . imitations of particular Arabic poems".[3] Not a few prose-writers of the twelfth and thirteenth centuries also wrote *maqāmas* in Hebrew; one of them, Judah ben Solomon al-Harizi (1165–1225) actually translated those of al-Harīrī in 1205. *Kalīla wa Dimna* was translated into Hebrew both by a certain Rabbi Joel and by Rabbi Eleazar ben Jacob (1283), who was also a *maqāma*-writer.

The Christians also, even when they were not won over to Islam, were attracted by Arab learning; annotations in Arabic on Latin texts show that their clerics were at home in the language. But the link between Arabic and the literatures that subsequently developed in Christian lands is not so precise or direct as it has been for Hebrew.

The clearest such link is the transmission of narratives. Early in the twelfth century Pedro Alfonso, a convert from Judaism baptized in 1106, put together thirty-three tales, Arab by origin or by transmission, which he translated into Latin and published under the title of *Disciplina clericalis*, indicating that they were intended for the edification of the literate. The book had a very wide diffusion in Europe, was translated into many languages, and echoes of it are found in such famous works as *Don Quixote* and the *Decameron*. Rabbi Joel's Hebrew version of *Kalīla wa Dimna* was also translated into Latin under the title of *Directorium Vitae Humanae* by John of Capua, himself a converted Jew.

Spanish narrative literature in particular owes a great deal of its initial impetus to early translations of three Oriental works that reached it at least in part through Arabic. The first was again *Kalīla wa Dimna*, translated from the Arabic by order of Alfonso X towards the middle of the thirteenth century. The other two are the *Syntipas*, also known as the *Sindibād-Nāme* and the *Sendebar*, another collection of tales of Indian origin, translated in 1253 under the title of *Libro de los engannos et los asayamientos de las mujeres*, and the story of *Barlaam and Josaphat*, based ultimately on the life of Buddha.

These stories echo and re-echo through the later literature of Spain and of other European countries, as do some of the tales from the *Arabian Nights*. Here and there other specific instances of indebtedness can be found; thus Turmeda's *Disputa de l'Ase* (1417), in which the Ass is made to rebut arguments for the alleged superiority of Man, closely follows one of the *Epistles of the Pure Brethren*, a tenth-century collection of treatises on science and philosophy. In his *Criticón*, Gracían also appears to have drawn in part on the same popular tale that Ibn-Ṭufayl used in his *Ḥayy ibn-Yaqẓān*.[4] An account of Muḥammad's ascent into heaven, the *Mi'rāj*, translated into Castilian by order of Alfonso X though now known only in French and Latin versions, may even have played a part in shaping Dante's imagination.[5]

The inspiration thus appears to be very largely from popular story-telling, but it has been suggested that the picaresque novel of the sixteenth and seventeenth centuries, which recounts sympathetically the rogueries and adventures of a low-born hero, may owe its existence to the *maqāma*.

Ribera has also conjectured the existence of an early popular epic, and sought to trace its possible influence on the *Chanson de Roland* and the *Poema del Cid*.

Much debated among Arabists and Romance scholars[6] has been the possible influence of Arabic poetry, more specifically of Andalusian strophic forms on the art of the juglares and troubadours, and hence on the whole lyrical tradition of Romance literatures.

Opportunities for such influence to be exerted were many where Christians and Muslims lived side by side and exchanges between courts were common; nor were contacts made in war necessarily barren in this respect. These opportunities are not merely matters of conjecture. Captive Morisco women singers are known to have performed in Christian courts; an illustration in Alfonso X's *Cantigas de Santa María* (1265) shows a Moor and a Christian singing together and accompanying themselves on identical lutes; and the Council of Valladolid in 1322 was condemning no imaginary evil when it forbade the employment of Muslim singers and performers in churches. One troubadour, García

Fernández, is known to have married a Morisco singer and to have moved between Christian and Muslim possessions in Spain.[7]

Significant similarities can in fact be detected between Andalusian and Romance lyric poetry. The most firmly demonstrable are those based on the structure of Andalusian strophic poetry. Indeed Guillaume IX appears to have incorporated some Arabic lines in his *Chanson 5*.[8] It is also argued, however, that there are similarities of substance especially in attitudes towards women and love, the troubadours perpetuating the amatory commonplaces of Andalusian poetry—the cruelty and tyranny of the beloved, the servility and sufferings of the lover, the intervention in a love intrigue of stock characters such as the confidant, the calumniator, the guardian—and all in all reflections of a more refined conception of love than was known in Europe until Ibn-Ḥazm.

That an Andalusian poetic tradition was one of several forces at work in the formative period of Romance literature it would be difficult to gainsay, especially when one remembers the undoubted contributions made by the culture of Islamic Spain in all other fields, including the closely allied one of music. The degree and extent of the influence exerted, however, can be determined only by detailed examinations of texts and close discussion of standards of comparisons on which there is as yet no agreement.[9] The argument cannot therefore be usefully summarised. Suffice it here to reproduce the view of Menéndez Pidal, a discriminating and well-informed Romance scholar: that Arab influence was one of several that can be detected in the earliest compositions of Provençal troubadours, notably Guillaume IX, Marcabru and Cercamon, but that it waned rapidly, surviving mostly in the popular anonymous songs of France and Italy; that it did not significantly penetrate Galician-Portuguese poetry except in Alfonso X's *Cantigas de Santa María*; that it was predominant in Castilian poetry until the sixteenth century when it was supplanted in all but the most vulgar forms, although traces of it subsist in the classical Spanish theatre which is rich in traditional songs.[10]

It yet remains to be stressed that what the Andalusians handed down to their Romance successors was not their classical tradition—not their monorhyme odes with their succession of conventional themes, not their trope-laden prose—but imaginative tales, strophic forms of poetry and perhaps the particularly refined lyricism of their love-songs. They were features remarkably close to those which have been held to distinguish their literature from that of their co-religionists of the East. They were also, in no small part, features that belonged to popular literature or derived from it.

This is consistent with a total picture of Islamic Spain in which the literature of the élite, strengthened by patronage, sought to perpetuate traditional standards no doubt valid but derived, and reaped the reward of steadfastness in glittering masterpieces. But co-existing with it, penetrating it only partially but more profoundly than in other lands where Arabic held sway, was another literature which was the natural expression of a population ethnically and culturally mixed, in which the Arab element gave and took, merged and moulded, was stimulated and in turn elaborated and developed. The fusion of these ethnic and cultural elements produced the distinctive features of Andalusia's literature; it also favoured their survival.

Andalusian literature was like the progeny of an expatriate aristocrat who had had two wives: one a free woman of his own race and background, the other a local bondwoman. The sons of the first wife shone best at court; those of the bondwoman were more adaptable, even when political change swept away their father's privilege.

4. *The Art of the Thirteenth and Fourteenth Centuries*

Despite the worsening political situation in the twelfth and thirteenth centuries the artistic tradition of Islamic Spain was still alive and indeed producing some of its greatest works. It may be regarded as having split up into two branches: Mudejar art, and the art of Granada (or Grenadine art).

The Mudejars, as already explained, were the Muslims who elected to remain in territories ruled by Christians. Their numbers were considerable in certain areas, and it was through this new form of association of Muslim and Christian that much of the culture of al-Andalus passed to Christian Spain, or rather was assimilated by Christian Spain in its expansion. This coming together of two societies in what is almost a single cultural organism is what is sometimes called "the Mudejar fact". Mudejar art, however, is not simply the art produced by the Mudejars, but rather the art arising out of this new cultural unity. It was an art which continued the tradition of Islamic art from the independent Muslim kingdoms, yet was genuinely at home in this new composite Christian-dominated society. So much was this the case that the craftsmen who carried out the work were sometimes Christian and sometimes Muslims from independent Granada, and yet the work had the Mudejar stamp; while Mudejar craftsmen who went elsewhere produced work in other styles.

Within the Mudejar style the experts distinguish "court Mudejar" from popular Mudejar. The former is exemplified above all in the Alcázar of Seville, and tends to follow Umayyad patterns. The latter has been described by Henri Terrasse as the national art of Spain at this period. It varied somewhat from region to region, since it incorporated aspects of the regional tradition. There are fine examples of Mudejar work in the churches of Toledo from the end of the twelfth century onwards. All this is extremely interesting in itself. From the point of view of the present survey, however, the great interest of Mudejar art is the evidence it provides for the symbiosis of the societies, resulting in the taking up into the life of the Christian kingdoms of much of the material and intellectual culture of al-Andalus.

The art of Granada is known to us especially from its greatest achievement, the Alhambra, though this was far from being the only product of the artistic activity of the Naṣrid kingdom. We can see in the Alhambra how the general outlook of the kingdom affected its art. It was a society on the defensive, conscious of being a bastion of Islam against a hostile world, and intent on preserving what it had inherited. In art this meant that it remained firmly within the earlier artistic tradition of al-Andalus, and introduced no novelty; that it rose to new heights of achievement was through the perfection of its craftsmanship.

The Alhambra is a complex of buildings on a spur of the Sierra Nevada above the town of Granada. Like other Moorish palaces it was also what would now be called "government offices". In addition it was a strong fortress. From the artistic point of view, however, interest centres on the palace proper, consisting of a comparatively small number of rooms and halls round two large and other smaller patios or courtyards. These were constructed mainly during the second two-thirds of the fourteenth century. The passion to cover whole surfaces with intricate finely-wrought decoration was given rein, with exquisite results. Full use was also made of the water, which was available in abundant supply from higher up the mountains, to place fountains, formal pools and vegetation in the courtyards—a great source of pleasure in the warm climate. The chief impression, however, is that of perfect ornamentation and perfect grace resting lightly on, even descending on, the slender columns.

This was an art that, in its exuberance, built for present enjoyment, and had no thought of creating enduring monuments. It used fragile materials superimposed on a basic structure that was of the slightest. It is mainly through a series of happy chances and the continuing care of successive generations that the Alhambra has been preserved for us. By the fifteenth century, however, the artistic impulse of the craftsmen of Granada was weakening doubtless as a result of the inward-turning attitude of the kingdom and its political decay. Before Naṣrid Granada was finally extinguished, its distinctive art was virtually defunct.

So it was that, partly through the actions of men (Christians) and partly through the natural processes of growth and decay, the art of Islamic Spain came to its end. The Spaniard of modern times has tended to regard the Moorish past of the country as something foreign to him, yet for those who have eyes to see the artist and craftsman of today still draw some of their inspiration from Islamic sources.

(11)

THE SIGNIFICANCE OF ISLAMIC SPAIN

1. *The Arab and Islamic Colony*

ONE of the lines of thought about Islamic Spain suggested at the beginning of this book is that which considers it as part of the great community of Muslims. It was a limb or organ of the vast cultural and religious body whose territories stretched from the Atlantic coasts of Spain and North Africa at first to Samarqand and the Punjab and latterly to the East Indian archipelago. What happened to the life of the body as it poured into this isolated limb? Were the forms of Islamic life suitable for the circumstances of the Iberian peninsula, or had there to be further measures of adaptation? Had the culture of al-Andalus anything to contribute to the culture of the heartlands? These are some of the questions now to be looked at again after this survey of the history of Islamic Spain. It should be clear by this time that, where there are so many gaps in our knowledge, any answers given can only be provisional.

To the student of culture one of the most interesting features of the Islamic society of the heartlands is the way in which the Muslim Arabs, through their language and religion, provided a mould into which could be poured most of the cultural heritage of the Fertile Crescent and neighbouring lands. The Arabs came from the desert and from towns largely dependent on the desert, and had thus a low standard of material culture, though they had attained—it may be claimed—a high degree of human excellence and of skill in personal relationships. The peoples they conquered in Iraq, Syria and Egypt had for centuries enjoyed a high level of material and intellectual culture, the latter including Greek philosophy and the Christian theology based on it. Yet it was the culture of the Arabs which became the matrix of the new Islamic civilisation, and all that was best in the older and higher culture was assimilated into the new culture.

In the case of Spain it has to be remembered that its main contacts with the heartlands were under the Umayyad caliphate (up to its demise in 750). After that time Islamic Spain was cut off in certain respects from the main centres of Islamic life, since these were under the rule of the 'Abbāsids, who had destroyed the Umayyads, whereas Spain continued under a branch of the Umayyad family for over 250 years longer. Now the Umayyad caliphate in the heartlands was characterised by the dominance of Arab elements rather than of the distinctively Islamic. The Umayyads were practising Muslims, but they did not show the same deference as the 'Abbāsids did to the self-appointed exponents of Islamic religion and religious law. In administration they attempted, though with increasing difficulty, to adapt Arab political ideas (derived from tribal institutions) to the running of an empire, whereas the 'Abbāsids openly leant on the Persian imperial traditions. The assimilation of Hellenistic thought by Muslims had begun under the Umayyads, but this had been almost exclusively in Iraq, and Syria had been unaffected.

Thus the culture of the first Muslims in al-Andalus was much more Arab than Islamic and the dominance of the Arab element continued to be characteristic. Evidence for this is the interest in Arabic poetry, in grammar, in the writing of commentaries on such typically Arab works as the *Maqāmāt* of al-Ḥarīrī, in details of Arab genealogy. The adoption of the Mālikite legal rite points in the same direction, for this was the most truly Arabian rite; the other main rites originated in Iraq where the intellectual milieu had been permeated by Hellenistic ideas. Similarly the philosophical theology of the East had no real foothold in Spain. This predominance of the Arab and anti-intellectual element makes it all the more remarkable that there should have been such a flowering of philosophy under the Almohads, and the reasons suggested above do not solve the mystery.

The evidence summarised in the body of the work tends to the conclusion that the Arab element continued to be dominant until the eleventh century, and that the Islamic element only exerted its full influence under the Almoravids and the Almohads. This was not because al-Andalus was entirely shut off from the heartlands. On the contrary, travel was usually easy, and at some periods it was normal for the scholars of al-Andalus to have studied in the great centres of Islamic learning such as Medina and Baghdad. The introduction of canons of taste from Baghdad by Ziryāb in the ninth century does not seem to have greatly affected the intellectual and religious life. More important was al-Ḥakam II's formation of a great library and the encouragement given about the same period to scholars from the heartlands to settle in al-Andalus. This created the foundation on which a more comprehensive structure of distinctively Islamic learning could be raised. The growth of specifically Islamic thought and feeling which this made possible was fostered by both Almoravids and Almohads because of their religious outlook.

In no part of the Islamic world after the first half-century or so did specifically Islamic ideas have much influence on the sphere of administration in general. The conception of the "holy war" could from time to time rouse the enthusiasm of the masses and swell the ranks of an army; and for this reason it was found useful by politicians. For the most part, however, the actual rulers of Islamic states found it necessary to follow secular traditions of governmental practice. The ʿAbbāsids had modelled their practice largely on pre-Islamic Persia, and something of this penetrated into the court-life and administration of al-Andalus. The next striking divergence of al-Andalus, however, from the theoretical Islamic norms is in the arrangements that came to be made with even greater frequency, whereby non-Muslim local rulers became tributary to Muslims and Muslim local rulers tributary to Christians. This appears to be an acceptance by the Muslims of local practices, perhaps specially appropriate to geographical conditions.

In this brief sketch of cultural developments in al-Andalus, these appear to have been determined (except in the political sphere) almost entirely by the culture of the heartlands, though by different strands at different times. Yet this is a case where appearances are deceptive, and where in fact Iberian influences are greater than at first sight they seem to be. One point that is clear is that nothing of the Christian intellectual culture of pre-Islamic Spain made any real contribution, despite the high level attained by Isidore of Seville and his school. On the contrary great numbers of the local inhabitants became Muslims, and in course of time were assimilated to the Arab section of the population. Even more surprising—and a point worthy of deep reflection—is the attraction of Arab culture for the indigenous inhabitants who remained Christian, and who because of this attraction were known as Mozarabs. One may surmise that perhaps, somehow or other, the Carthaginian heritage influenced them in this way. Certainly much of the culture of al-Andalus (apart from specifically religious dogmas) was shared by all the inhabitants of al-Andalus of whatever racial origin and religious confession. It was from popular aspects of this amalgam (it seems) that the new poetic forms developed which were one of the chief original contributions of al-Andalus to the heartlands (though the scholars working in the traditional disciplines also made contributions of value).

Indeed, the more these matters are reflected on, the more it is clear that there was a genuine symbiosis of indigenous and adventitious elements of population with their respective cultures. Many of the outward forms which are most easily apprehended by the modern scholar were contributed by the Arabs, and also something of the spiritual drive. Yet the creative energies which produced the great aesthetic achievements in architecture, literature and other arts, seem to have come at least as much from the Iberian element or some section of it. Here we are up against one of the great mysteries. Just as the Persian genius found in Islam something which fertilised it and enabled it to flower luxuriantly, so also it seems to have been the case with the Iberians.

It should further be kept in mind that there may have been Berber contributions to the cultural amalgam, but these are hard to detect. The most obvious would be an interest in the saint or charismatic leader, which has long been a feature of North African religion. This, however, as explained above, could not have much influence in Spain because of the dependence of the Berbers on the Muslim rulers. It contributed to the set of ideas underlying the Almoravid and Almohad movements, but the extension of the culture of al-Andalus into North Africa under the dominion of these movements suggests that the Berbers had little of their own to contribute. In any case, a discussion of the Berbers would belong rather to the study of North Africa.

2. *The Stimulation of Christian Spain and Europe*

A second group of questions is concerned with the relation of Islamic Spain to Christian Spain and more generally to Christian Europe. With regard to Christian Spain in particular there is little doubt about the fact. Somehow or other it was the necessity of struggling for very existence against the Muslims that made Christian Spain great. In the Reconquista Spain found its soul. The difficulty is to explain just how this came about. A view commonly held has been that there was an essential continuity between the Catholic Spain of Visigothic times and that of Ferdinand and Isabella. The difficulty about this view is that the kingdom of the Asturias, which was the centre from which the Reconquista began, was not part of Visigothic Spain in any important sense, but rather a rebel on its borders. Much nearer to the truth seems to be the view of Américo Castro in *The Structure of Spanish History*—a view which is summed up in the words: "Christian Spain 'became'—emerged into being—as she incorporated and grafted into her living process what she was compelled to by her interaction with the Moslem world" (p. 96).

The fire of the Reconquista was certainly kindled in the Asturias first and then in the other little northern kingdoms. To begin with, however, it was not so much a hope of reconquest as merely a fierce desire for independence; nor did it arise consciously from zeal for the propagation of Christianity and its defence against Muslims. Care must be taken not to read back into the past what belongs to later centuries. Time and time again the actors on both sides are found paying scant attention to the differences of religion. It seems to have been about the middle of the eleventh century before the movement of expansion of the northern kingdoms became consciously identified with the extension of Christendom; and it was a little later that the Muslims became consciously defenders of the territories where Islam was dominant.

In their bitter struggle, however, first for independence and then for the extension of their power, the men of the north turned more and more to the Christian faith. In particular they found in the cult of Santiago (Saint James of Compostella) a source of supernatural power to sustain them in trials and give them hope of ultimate victory. At the same time they could not afford to neglect the material foundations of military victory; and as far as they could they took over the weapons and techniques which seemed to give the Muslims superiority. Along with these they adopted many other aspects of the superior civilisation with which they were at grips. The process of assimilation was hastened by the practice, begun at least as early as the tenth century, of settling Mozarabs from the Muslim territories in waste lands on the borders of the Christian domains. Gradually these people and their culture became an integral part of the Christian kingdoms. At a later stage a second factor still further promoted assimilation—the existence of large bodies of Muslims, the Mudejars, within the Christian states. As the Christians from the north became familiar with Toledo (after 1085), with Cordova (after 1236), with Seville (after 1248) and with many lesser Islamic cities, they accepted the way of life which had developed in al-Andalus—all except its religious aspect. Thus the will to reconquest—the will to be Christian Spain—found in the culture of al-Andalus the elements which, compounded, gave it its outward embodiment; but these elements were far from foreign, since they were taken from the symbiosis of Arabo-Islamic and Iberian societies.

This complexity of cultural relationships also underlies the phenomenon of the Troubadours and some of the conceptions associated with chivalry. It is impossible to say that any particular feature is due either to the Orient or to Europe, for there had been such a fusion of the two strands that it is no longer possible to make an absolute distinction between them. Yet somehow or other in this new unity there was creative fire, which kindled further fires.

Likewise it was through the symbiosis or cultural fusion that it was possible for Greek philosophy—both translations of Greek books and original works in Arabic of Muslim thinkers—to reach Christian Europe. There was no "iron curtain" between Christian Toledo and Islamic Cordova in the later twelfth century when Averroes was at the height of his power; and the thought of the great Aristotelian penetrated more easily into Christian Europe than into the Islamic heartlands, and constituted a large part of the stimulus which provoked the greatest intellectual achievement of medieval Christendom, the philosophy of Saint Thomas Aquinas.

While a long list can be made of particular things which Christian Europe owes to al-Andalus—a list which goes from pieces of scientific knowledge and philosophical conceptions through techniques of applied science to aspects of form in literature and the visual arts—it is important not to lose sight of the general situation. Islamic culture was the main higher culture with which Western Christendom was in direct contact for much of the period under review; and behind this culture was the most powerful political organisation of which Western Christendom had experience. It was really only in the period of the crusades that there was any close contact with Eastern (Byzantine) Christendom—and the very conception of "crusade" probably owes much to the *jihād* or "holy war" of the Muslims. Because of this special relationship of Western Christendom to the Islamic world—a relationship of which the focal point was Spain—it was only natural that the Christians should feel both strong attraction and strong repulsion. Islam was at one and the same time the great enemy and the great source of higher material and intellectual culture. Would it be fanciful to see in this a parallel to the relationship to contemporary Europe of the new nations of Asia and Africa? If there is a parallel, then the European who is able to enter imaginatively into his own history, can experience something of what it feels like to be a member of one of these new nations.

3. *The Intrinsic Greatness of Islamic Spain*

The third and most difficult set of questions is that concerned with Islamic Spain in itself. In particular there is the question whether it has an intrinsic greatness or whether its reputation is a reflection, through the centuries, of the outward magnificence which impressed the somewhat backward medieval Christians.

There can be no doubt that the Europeans were impressed in this way. Some of the contributions of al-Andalus to the life of Europe have just been described. As the point has been made—more graphically—by Américo Castro (p. 87), "those victorious armies (*sc.* in 1248) could not repress their astonishment upon beholding the grandeur of Seville; the Christians had never possessed anything similar in art, economic splendour, civil organisation, technology, and scientific and literary productivity". When allowance is made for all this, however, and when we admit that we are still in part influenced by a cultural memory of former admiration for material luxury and intellectual sublimity, are there any reasons left for considering the Islamic period of Spanish history as being among the great ages of mankind?

One test would be to ask how many of the writers and thinkers of al-Andalus are worthy of a place among the classics of the "one world" into which we are moving. (This is, of course, a rough and ready test, which begs many questions.) There are undoubtedly a few names which at once suggest themselves as possible. Most obvious, perhaps, is Averroes, partly because of his influence on Christian philosophy, though he is worthy of a place in his own right. Although it is somewhat slight, the charm of *Ḥayy ibn-Yaqẓān* by Ibn-Ṭufayl gives it a claim to be among the immortals. Ibn-Khaldūn, if he can be reckoned as belonging to the tradition of al-Andalus, has also a place;

but Ibn-Ḥazm is rather on the border-line, since his works are closely linked with the whole dogmatic intellectual milieu and have less of a universal quality. Among the poets it is doubtful if any can be said to be of universal appeal; but perhaps some of the mystics, like Muḥyī-d-Dīn ibn-al-ʿArabī, will be included in the world's pantheon of mystic "saints". Thus al-Andalus has a few men of the very first rank; and behind these one can discern many others in the second rank—of whom a few are known fairly well—whose achievements in the strange business of living were of no little merit. The life of al-Andalus is indeed a noble facet of the total experience of mankind.

Apart from literature there is also the loveliness of the Moorish buildings that have been preserved. There is something of transcendent value in a beautiful object; and it may be argued that a civilisation which can produce such objects must have a quality of greatness. In general this argument may be allowed to be sound. Yet it is instructive to contrast our attitude to the Parthenon with our attitude to the Alhambra. Many people who admire both would be inclined to say that they see in the Parthenon a thing of beauty which is at the same time an expression of the Greek spirit, whereas the Alhambra is for them just a thing of intrinsic beauty without any reference to the culture which produced it.

This contrast is worth looking at more closely. It is indeed natural that we should have a much greater appreciation of Greek culture than of Moorish culture. The former—or at least a selection from it—is part of our own heritage, part of the tradition into which we enter; but the latter, for all that it has contributed to the culture of Europe, was in its essence something alien, the great enemy, to be feared even in the moment of admiration. Our inherited "image" of Islam was framed in the twelfth and thirteenth centuries under the domination of this fear of the Saracen; and even now few western Europeans can regard

Islam with impartiality. Yet should our appreciation of a beautiful object be affected by our lack of appreciation of the culture from which it springs? May it not, on the contrary, be the case that appreciation of a beautiful object is able to provide a key to the appreciation of the alien culture? May it not even be that the beautiful object is the measure and the validation of the culture? Because of lovely buildings like the Great Mosque of Cordova and the Alhambra of Granada must not the culture of Islamic Spain be a great culture?

This point will bear expansion. There is an obvious difference between the Parthenon and the Alhambra. When we admire the Parthenon, we mainly do so from outside, whereas it is only from inside that the Alhambra can be admired. This has nothing to do with the contrast of religious and secular purposes, for it is also true that the glories of the Great Mosque of Cordova are mainly within. It has further been suggested that the slender pillars of the Alhambra with the elaborate and massive overstructure express the descent from a supernal realm of that which is of eternal value and significance, whereas other buildings express rather man's attempt to rise up to heaven. Now suggestions of this type may be multiplied and elaborated, and some will no doubt win wider approval than others. Even the best, however, is bound to be to a great extent inadequate, for the appreciation of beauty can never be reduced to conceptual terms. Nevertheless, if there is something in the above suggestion which even distantly approximates to the essence of the appreciated beauty, then man in the Western-European tradition who finds the beauty of the Alhambra touching a responsive chord in himself is acknowledging the high intrinsic worth of this expression of the soul of Islamic Spain, and providing himself with a key to a deeper understanding of this whole culture.

NOTES

(1)

THE MUSLIM CONQUEST

Abbreviations

EI[1], *EI*[2], *EI(S)*: *Encyclopaedia of Islam*, four volumes and supplement.

GAL, *GALS*: *Geschichte der Arabischen Literatur*.

1. For a general account of Arab expansion, cf. Bernard Lewis, *The Arabs in History*, London, 1950, chs. 3, 4.
2. The best and most complete account is the composite volume with the separate title *España visigoda*, which constitutes volume III of the *Historia de España* directed by Ramón Menéndez Pidal (Madrid, 1940). This contains an important section on Visigothic art and is lavishly illustrated. In English the doctoral dissertation of Aloysius K. Ziegler, entitled *Church and State in Visigothic Spain* (Washington, 1930), is to be highly recommended. The first chapter, pp. 1-25, of *Islam d'Espagne* by Henri Terrasse (cf. p. 188) is also worthy of mention.
3. Detailed justification of the statements here, will be found in Lévi-Provençal, *Histoire de l'Espagne musulmane*, i. 8-34 (cf. p. 186 below).

(2)

THE PROVINCE OF THE DAMASCUS CALIPHATE

1. Cf. Américo Castro, *The Structure of Spanish History*, 77-9, and contrast Lévi-Provençal, *Histoire*, i. 66, 68, which appears to show that Pelayo and Alfonso I were of Visigothic descent.

(3)

THE INDEPENDENT UMAYYAD EMIRATE

1. The form (in Latin) *muztarabes* is quoted from a document of Alfonso VI dated 1101 by Isidro de las Cagigas, *Los Mozárabes* (Madrid, 1947), i, 72 n. 31.
2. The continuance of Latin or Romance speech is emphasised by Armand Abel in *Unity and Variety in Muslim Civilization*, ed. G. E. von Grunebaum, Chicago, 1955, 207.
3. The word "feudalism" is used here in a loose sense by a historian of Islam to indicate relationships which to his inexpert eye are more like European feudalism than anything in the Islamic world. What is here said is therefore compatible with the common view of historians of Europe that in Spain there was no feudalism in the strict sense.

(4)

THE GRANDEUR OF THE UMAYYAD CALIPHATE

1. Cf. Montgomery Watt, *Islam and the Integration of Society*, London, 1961, 158 f.
2. Cf. Montgomery Watt, *Islamic Philosophy and Theology*, Edinburgh, 1962, 100-103.
3. *The Structure of Spanish History*, 167-9; cf. 149.
4. For this evidence of language see Castro, *Structure of Spanish History*, 96-100; cf. T. W. Arnold and A. Guillaume (edd.), *The Legacy of Islam*, Oxford, 1931, 19-24.
5. H. Heaton, *Economic History of Europe*, 2nd ed., New York, 1948, 78.
6. Cf. T. W. Arnold, *The Preaching of Islam*, 3rd ed., London, 1935, 131-4.
7. *Zeitschrift der deutschen morgenländischen Gesellschaft*, liii (1899), 601-20; the two judges are on p. 605, the phrase used being *shadīd al-ʿaṣabiyya li-ʾl-muwalladīn*. In n. 2 the figure should be "1147".

8. Alvar, *Indiculus luminosus*, § 35; quoted from Arnold, *Preaching of Islam*, 137 f.
9. Dr E. Bosworth calls attention to a similar adaptation in India in the eleventh and twelfth centuries, where the population was too extensive to convert (private communication).
10. Cf. Montgomery Watt, *Muslim Intellectual*, Edinburgh, 1963, 88-108.

(5)

CULTURAL ACHIEVEMENTS UNDER THE UMAYYADS

1. Cf. Montgomery Watt, *Integration*, 199-209. For a general account of Islamic law, cf. N. J. Coulson, *Islamic Law*, Edinburgh, 1964.
2. E.g. al-Ghāzī ibn-Qays (Ibn-al-Faraḍī, no. 1013).
3. Cf. J. Schacht, *The Origins of Muhammadan Jurisprudence*, Oxford, 1950, 288 f., 311-14.
4. M. Talbi, "Kairouan et le malikisme espagnol", in *Études Lévi-Provençal*, Paris, 1962, i.317-37; cf. R. Brunschvig in *Al-Andalus*, xv (1950), 401. The books were the *Asadiyya* of Asad ibn-al-Furāt and the *Mudawwana* of Saḥnūn (d. 854), the latter being by far the more important.
5. Cf. *Islamic Philosophy and Theology*, ch. 7.
6. M. Asín Palacios, *Obras escogidas*, i (Madrid, 1946), 1-216, "Ibn Masarra y su escuela"; Appendix II (179-84) deals with the first Muʿtazilites in Spain.
7. Spanish tr. by J. Ribera, *Historia de los Jueces de Córdoba por Aljoxani*, Madrid, 1914.
8. *Moorish Poetry*, introd., xiii.
9. See Ch. 4, n. 8 (and p. 56).
10. "Les Méthodes de réalisation artistique des peuples de l'Islam", *Syria* (1921), 19.
11. What is said in this section (and the others dealing with art) follows closely the treatment of Henri Terrasse in *Islam d'Espagne* (see Bibliography).
12. *Op. cit.* 101.
13. ʿUthmān ibn-al-Muthannā (Ibn-al-Faraḍī, no. 889) and Faraj ibn-Sallām (*ibid.* no. 1036).

14. *Ibid.* no. 199; R. Guest, *The Governors and Judges of Egypt*, 548. An example of how far Spanish Muslims had assimilated the ideals of pre-Islamic Arabs will be found in A. Abel's article in *Unity and Variety*, ed. von Grunebaum, 214.
15. Abū-'l-Ḥasan al-Anṭākī (Ibn-al-Faraḍī, no. 132; as-Subkī, ii. 313; *Shadharāt adh-Dhahab*, iii. 90); he is said to have lived from what his slave-girl earned by spinning, but no date is assigned to this. For the other scholar see Ibn-al-Faraḍī, no. 933.
16. *Histoire*, ii. 147 f.

(6)

THE COLLAPSE OF ARAB RULE

1. Cf. A. Castro, *The Structure of Spanish History*, 158: "The damage wrought by this Islamic thunderbolt increased the faith in the holy relic, so holy that not even Almanzor himself had succeeded in destroying it".
2. Cf. *Islam and the Integration of Society*, ch. 5; and p. 43 above.
3. For a general picture of conditions a little later, cf. Lévi-Provençal, "Mémoires de ʿAbdullah . . . de Grenade", *Al-Andalus*, iii, iv (1935, 1936).
4. Cf. *EI*², art. ʿAbbādids.
5. Cf. *EI*², art. Djahwarids.
6. There has been much discussion of the historical basis of the legends clustering round the Cid, but this belongs primarily to the history of Christian Spain. The best work on the subject is R. Menéndez Pidal, *El España de Mio Cid*, 1929, etc. English tr. *The Cid and his Spain*, London, 1934, etc.

(7)

THE BERBER EMPIRES—THE ALMORAVIDS

1. The fullest account is that of Alfred Bel in *La Religion musulmane en Berbérie*, I, Paris, 1938, 211-31 (who had previously been responsible for the article "Almoravides" in *EI*¹; the corresponding article in *EI*² will appear as "Murābiṭūn").

2. *GALS*, i. 660. "Fāsī" means "coming from Fez".
3. Cf. A. González Palencia, *Historia de la España musulmana*,[4] Madrid, 1945, 96-8.

(8)

THE BERBER EMPIRES—THE ALMOHADS

1. General references: I. Goldziher, "Materialien zur Kentniss der Almohaden-Bewegung", *Zeitschrift der deutschen morgenländischen Gesellschaft*, xli (1887), 30-140; also his "Introduction" to J. D. Luciani, *Le Livre de Moḥammed ibn Toumert*, Algiers, 1903; these are still unsurpassed. Articles: "Ibn Tūmart" in *EI*(*S*); "'Abd al-Mu'min" in *EI*[2]; "Muwaḥḥidūn" (not yet available) in *EI*[2]; R. Brunschvig, "Sur la doctrine du Mahdi Ibn Tūmart", *Ignace Goldziher Memorial Volume* (ed. S. Löwinger), ii. 1-13. A. Huici Miranda, *Historia política del imperio almohade*, Tetuan, 1956–7.
2. Cf. J. F. P. Hopkins, "The Almohade Hierarchy", *Bulletin of the School of Oriental and African Studies*, xvi (1954), 93-112.
3. A. Castro, *Structure of Spanish History*, 130 ff., esp. 167-9.

(9)

CULTURAL GREATNESS IN POLITICAL DECLINE

1. G. Marçais, *La Berbérie musulmane et l'Orient au Moyen Âge*, 12.
2. See Nykl, *Hispano-Arabic Poetry*, 135-6.
3. *Ibid.*, 229-30.
4. See a somewhat different translation in Nykl, p. 228. Najd is the central upland of Arabia, Tihāma the coastal strip. It was a widespread convention in Arabic poetry to speak of the loved woman in the masculine gender.
5. Pérès, *Poésie andalouse*, 424.
6. García Gómez, *Poemas arábigoandaluces*, 43-4.
7. *Op. cit.* pp. 465-6.

8. *Op. cit.*, particularly pp. 473-5.
9. In intro. of Ibn Khallikān's *Biographical Dictionary* I (Paris, 1842), p. xxxv.
10. See Pérès, *op. cit.* pp. 159-60.
11. The lines are by Ibn-Quzmān (d. 1160), the vizier of al-Mutawakkil of Badajoz. Nykl gives a different translation in *Hispano-Arabic Poetry*, p. 302.
12. García Gómez, *Poesía arábigoandaluza*, pp. 30-31.
13. This is, in substance, the hypothesis first put forward by Ribera and taken up with modifications by García Gómez in "Sobre un posible tercer tipo de poesía arábigoandaluza", *Estudios dedicados a Menéndez Pidal*, II (Madrid, 1951), pp. 397-408, to account for the appearance of strophic forms. It does not seem far-fetched to extend it to the modest changes observable in conventional poetry.
14. See S. M. Stern, *Les Chansons mozarabes*, xiii-xvii.
15. *Dār aṭ-Ṭirāz* (Damascus, 1949), 37.
16. See García Gómez, "Sobre un posible tercer tipo de poesía arábigoandaluza", 400-1.
17. These non-classical forms were first brought to the attention of Orientalists by von Hammer in "Notice: Sur dix formes de versification arabe dont une couple à peine était connue jusqu'à présent des orientalistes européens", *Journal Asiatique*, 3e série, Tome VIII (août, 1839), 162-71. More recently, a great deal of information scattered through the sources has been usefully brought together by ʿAlī al-Khāqānī in *Funūn al-Adab ash-Shaʿbī* (Baghdad, 1962).
18. See Nykl, *Hispano-Arabic Poetry*, p. 269.
19. *Poesía arábigoandaluza*, 43-9.
20. Almost certainly not the same man as the one mentioned in n. 11, but there is some confusion in the sources.
21. *Poésie andalouse* 24-5.
22. The word is usually, justifiably, translated "assembly", but it can also be used of a dramatic situation, a prowess, a harangue, etc. See R. Blachère, "Étude sémantique sur le nom maqâma", *Mashriq*, 47 (1953), 646-52.
23. The entire output of Andalusian *maqāmas* has yet to be adequately studied. The material available has been conveniently

indicated by Dr. Aḥmad Mukhtār al-ʿAbbādī in "Maqāmat al-ʿId . . .", *Revista del Instituto Egipcio de Estudios Islámicos*, 2 (1954), 159-73.

24. The broad question of Muslim influences on Dante was first raised by Miguel Asín Palacios in *La escatología musulmana en la Divina Comedia* (Madrid, 1919) and gave rise to a lively polemic, reviewed by Asín Palacios in the second edition of his book (Madrid, 1943). A direct link between al-Maʿarrī and Dante is, however, entirely conjectural, and receives little credence either from Orientalists or from modern Arab scholars—see ʿAbd-ar-Razzāq Ḥumayda, *Fī ʿl-Adab al-Muqāran* (Cairo, 1948), 91-101. A likelier channel through which Muslim eschatological ideas may have reached Dante is mentioned p. 159 below.
25. *Op. cit.* 37-8.
26. For Ibn-Ḥazm see article in *EI*. Also: I. Goldziher, *Die Ẓâhiriten* Leipzig, 1884, esp. 116-72, which discusses his jurisprudence and theology. M. Asín Palacios, *Abenházam de Córdoba, y su historia crítica de las ideas religiosas*, five vols., Madrid, 1927–32, has (in the first vol.) a useful discussion of his life and of his thought in general; the rest is a translation or summary, at times misleading, of his book *Al-Fiṣal* on the sects. The important study by Roger Arnaldez, *Grammaire et théologie chez Ibn Ḥazm de Cordoue*, Paris, 1956, links up his theological position with particular views about the nature of language.
27. Lévi-Provençal, *Histoire*, iii. 182.
28. (*Ṭawq al-ḥamāma*), translated by A. J. Arberry, London, 1953. This is to be preferred to the earlier English translation by A. Nykl. There are also translations in several other European languages.
29. For a list of his works cf. *GALS*, i. 692-7.
30. *GAL*, i. 453 f.; *GALS*, i. 628 f.
31. *GAL*, i. 455 f.; *GALS*, i. 630-2; Tor Andrae, *Die Person Muhammeds in Lehre und Glauben seiner Gemeinde*, Stockholm, 1918, 60, 112, 118 f., 131, 147-50, 204-12, etc. (the *Shifā'* has been an important source for Andrae of earlier views); Andrae is mistaken in calling ʿIyāḍ an Ashʿarite—it was as Mālikite that al-Bāqillānī was his "*Gesinnungsgenosse*".

32. There is a full account in R. Brunschvig, "Averroès juriste", *Études Lévi-Provençal*, i (Paris, 1962), 35-68.
33. A conspectus is given by Charles Pellat, "The Origin and Development of Historiography in Muslim Spain", in B. Lewis and P. M. Holt (edd.), *Historians of the Middle East*, London, 1962, 118-25.
34. Ibn Khaldūn, *The Muqaddimah, an Introduction to History*, tr. by Franz Rosenthal, 3 vols. London, 1958, p. xxxvi.
35. *The Rule of the Solitary*, ed. and tr. by M. Asín Palacios, Madrid, 1946. English tr. of first section by D. M. Dunlop in *Journal of the Royal Asiatic Society*, 1945, 61-81.
36. For al-Ghazālī see *Islamic Philosophy and Theology*, ch. 13; and Watt, *Muslim Intellectual*, Edinburgh, 1963.
37. Translated by S. Ockley as *The Improvement of Human Reason*, London, 1708; revised by A. S. Fulton, London, 1929. Also by P. Brönnle, as *The Awakening of the Soul*, London, 1904. See also *GAL*, i. 602 f.; *GALS*, i. 831 f.
38. There is an excellent English translation by Simon van den Bergh, with the title: *Averroes' Tahafut al-Tahafut* (*The Incoherence of the Incoherence*), London, 1954 (Gibb Memorial Series). Another useful translation is *Ibn Rushd* (*Averroes*) *on the Harmony of Religion and Philosophy*, by George F. Hourani, London, 1962. For further references see Watt, *Islamic Philosophy and Theology*, 144 f.
39. Cf. *GAL*, i. 611; *GALS*, i. 844.
40. M. Asín Palacios, "El místico Abū-l-ʿAbbās ibn al-ʿArīf de Almería . . .", *Obras escogidas*, i (Madrid, 1946), 217-42. The form ʿIrrīf is preferable to ʿArīf according to *GAL*, i. 559, where there is also a notice of Ibn-Barrajān.
41. *Obras escogidas*, i. 145-51. In general cf. A. J. Arberry, *Sufism*, London, 1950, 97-101; A. E. Affifi, *The Mystical Philosophy of Muhyid Din Ibnul ʿArabi*, Cambridge, 1939; *Tarjumān al-Aswāq*, tr. by R. A. Nicholson, London, 1911; H. Corbin, *L'Imagination créatrice dans le çoufisme d'Ibn ʿArabī*, Paris, 1958; A. Jeffery, "Ibn al-ʿArabī's Shajarat al-Kawn" (translation), *Studia Islamica*, x. 43-77, xi. 113-160.
42. *GALS*, ii. 358: M. Asín Palacios, "Un precursor hispano-musulman de San Juan de la Cruz", *Obras escogidas*, i. 243-326

(from *Al-Andalus*, i [1933]. 7-79); *Lettres de direction spirituelle*, tr. P. Nwyia, Beirut, 1958.

(10)

THE LAST OF ISLAMIC SPAIN

1. Illustrative passages are to be found in *Khulāṣat Taʾrīkh Tūnus* by Ḥasan aṣ-Ṣumādiḥī (Tunis, 1925), pp. 141 ff. (reference communicated by G. M. Wickens).
2. Muḥammad Mzālī, "Al-Buṭūla kamā yuṣawwiruhā 'l-adab al-ʿarabī fī 'l-Andalus wa shamāl Ifrīqyā", *al-Fikr*, v. 4, n. 5 (Feb. 1959), 22-33.
3. S. M. Stern, "ʿĀŝiqayn Iʿtanaqā—An Arabic Muwaŝŝaḥ and its Hebrew Imitations", *al-Andalus*, 28, 1 (1963), 155-70.
4. See Angel González Palencia, *Historia de la literatura arábigo-española*, 334-48.
5. See Enrico Cerulli, *Libro della Scala e la questione delle fonti arabo-spagnole della Divina Commedia* (Vatican, 1949), and Francesco Gabrieli, "Ḍawʾ jadīd ʿalā Dāntī wa 'l-Islām", *Revue de l'Académie Arabe de Damas*, 33, Pt. 1 (Jan. 1958), 36-55.
6. Among those who put forward the view that Arabic has been influential are P. Juan Andre, Ribera, Burdach, Singer, Mulertt, Nykl and Menéndez Pidal. Among those who favour rival theories are Gaston Paris, Jeanroy, Pillet, Schrötter and Vossler.
7. Aḥmad Luṭfī ʿAbd al-Badīʿ, "At-Trūbādūr Gharsiyah Firnandith", *Revista del Instituto Egipcio de Estudios Islámicos*, ii, 1-2, (1954), 85-92.
8. See Lévi-Provençal, "Arabica Occidentalia, II", *Arabica*, i (1954), 201-11.
9. If, for example, the essentials of the *zajal* are reduced to stanzas with the rhyme scheme bbbA, cccA, etc., parallels will be found as far afield as in Scottish and Irish ballads; see González Palencia, *op. cit.* 357 ff. Nykl and Menéndez Pidal, however, base their conclusions on far more complex analogies.
10. *Poesía árabe y poesía europea*, 68-78.

BIBLIOGRAPHY

A. DETAILED HISTORY

For the period up to 1031 there may be said to be a standard historiographical tradition, that established by Reinhardt Dozy and continued by Évariste Lévi-Provençal. Both did a vast amount of work in making available the basic source-material, including that for the later period. Dozy's *Histoire des musulmans d'Espagne, 711–1110* was first published at Leiden in 1861, and translated into English as *Spanish Islam* (London, 1913). Lévi-Provençal brought out a revised edition in 1932, but later decided that an entirely new work was needed. Unfortunately only three volumes of his *Histoire de l'Espagne musulmane* had appeared before his death. These take the story to 1031, and completely supersede the earlier works mentioned. Their full bibliographical references are indispensable for the serious student, and make it unnecessary to include references in the earlier part of the present survey. Since the standard view of the earlier history of Islamic Spain is thus mainly the work of two closely associated men, it may be that when some scholar with a different perspective familiarises himself with all the material the general line of interpretation will be modified.

For the period after 1031 there is no such historiographical tradition and no single work covering the period in any detail. This is a serious gap in modern historical studies, and is reflected in the sections on this period in large composite works and in the smaller popular books on Islamic Spain. For the rest of the eleventh century there is the third volume of Lévi-Provençal's revision of Dozy, but he would probably have altered the treatment considerably in the projected fourth volume of his own history. The Almohad period is dealt with in some detail by Ambrosio Huici Miranda in his *Historia política del imperio almohade*, Tetuan, 1956–7. There are numerous works in Spanish on particular matters, usually from a specifically Christian angle; for example, the four volumes of A. González Palencia on *Los Mozárabes de Toledo en los siglos XII y XIII*, Madrid, 1926–30.

Of shorter popular works one of the best is that by the last author, entitled *Historia de la España musulmana*, fourth revised edition, Barcelona, 1945; but this is now beginning to be out of date. *A Political History of Muslim Spain* (Dacca, 1961), by a Pakistani scholar S. M. Imamuddin, is competent but apparently based on the older work of Lévi-Provençal, and rather fades away when that ceases. Much better than either of these, though not strictly a history, is *Islam d'Espagne* by Henri Terrasse (to be mentioned in section B). Philip K. Hitti in his *History of the Arabs* (London, 1937, etc., various editions) devotes most of Part IV (over a hundred pages) to Spain, and is specially strong on the intellectual contributions. In the large composite *Historia de España* under the direction of R. Menéndez Pidal, vols. IV and V are simply translations of Lévi-Provençal and the later volumes are not yet published.

There are two further ways in which the gaps still left may sometimes be filled. There are many articles concerning Islamic Spain, sometimes containing material not otherwise available in European languages, in *The Encyclopaedia of Islam*: four volumes and supplement, Leiden, 1913–42; second edition, vol. 1, Leiden and London, 1960, continuing. Articles of religious interest from the first edition, often with some revision, were reprinted in a separate volume as *Handwörterbuch des Islam* (1941) and *A Shorter Encyclopaedia of Islam* (1953). There is naturally a tendency for the older articles to be out of date. In the second place there is a vast number of articles in periodicals of all kinds; and a classified list of these is to be found in J. D. Pearson's *Index Islamicus*, 1906–55 (Cambridge, 1958) and the first supplement, 1956–60. The sections dealing with Islamic Spain are XXXV (history) and XXXVII, h (literature).

B. GENERAL INTERPRETATIONS

There have been vehement debates within Spain and beyond its frontiers about the general interpretation of Spanish history and the significance of the Moorish period for the whole. The romantic aspect of Moorish Spain seems to have caught the imagination of Europe as a result of the publication of *Tales of the Alhambra* by Washington Irving in 1832. In this spirit Stanley Lane-Poole, who admired the

Arabs but disliked contemporary Spaniards, thought Spain's greatness was due to the Moors and that her decadence began when she expelled them (*The Moors in Spain*, London, 1888). Catholic Spaniards, on the other hand, have sometimes tended to regard the period of Islamic domination as a mere interruption in the continuing life of a single entity, Catholic Spain. With many refinements this is the idea behind the writings of C. Sanchez Albornoz. A more exciting and apparently more balanced treatment of the complex questions at issue—and one more congenial to the Islamist—is that of Américo Castro in *The Structure of Spanish History* (tr. by E. L. King, Princeton, 1954), a revision of his *España en su historia: cristianos, moros y judios* (Buenos Ayres, 1948). His general thesis is that there was no continuity between Visigothic Spain and later Christian Spain, but that the latter was something new which was born and grew up in the mixed culture (largely Arab) which developed under the Muslims.

Of books specially devoted to Islamic Spain one is outstanding: *Islam d'Espagne, une rencontre de l'Orient et de l'Occident* by Henri Terrasse, Paris, 1958. The author's primary interest is in the history of art and archaeology, and he makes full use of materials from this sphere in putting forward a view of Islamic Spain which is roughly that of Américo Castro. Valuable, too, are the three lectures, first delivered in Egypt in 1938, in which Lévi-Provençal shares his general reflections on the subject to which he had given his life: *La Civilisation arabe en Espagne, vue générale* (new edition, Paris, 1948).

C. LITERATURE

References in Section "A" to the *Encyclopaedia of Islam* and to J. D. Pearson's *Index Islamicus* are equally relevant here. There are also important contributions to the understanding of Spanish-Arabic literature scattered in the historical works of Dozy and Lévi-Provençal, and in Julián Ribera y Tarragó's *Disertaciones y opúsculos*, 2 vols. (Madrid, 1928).

The fundamental work for all Islamic source material in Arabic is Carl Brockelmann's *Geschichte der Arabischen Literatur*, consisting of two original volumes (second edition, Leiden, 1943, 1949) and three supplementary volumes (1937–42). This work lists all the manuscripts of Islamic Arabic works known to Western scholars up to the time of publication, as well as the printed editions. It also gives the dates of each author, where known, and a few biographical details, with references to notices in Arabic biographical dictionaries and to modern books and articles. The primary division is into chronological periods. In each period there are subdivisions according to subject, but each author appears only in one place.

Not to be overlooked are the sections on Spain in general histories of Arabic literature, notably: Reynold A. Nicholson, *Literary History of the Arabs* (second edition, Cambridge, 1930), pp. 405-41; Sir Hamilton Gibb, *Arabic Literature, an Introduction* (second edition, Oxford, 1963), pp. 108-17, 136-41; Francesco Gabrieli, *Storia della letteratura araba* (Milan, 1951), pp. 163-76, 236-8, 247-54, 262-269; J.-M. Abd-el-Jalil, *Histoire de la littérature arabe* (second edition, Paris, 1960), pp. 191-203.

The one comprehensive book on Spanish-Arabic literature is *Historia de la literatura arábigo-española*, by Angel González Palencia (second edition, Madrid, 1945); it sums up in a convenient form the results obtained by scholars, mostly Spanish and French, until twenty years ago.

On poetry, Adolf Friedrich von Schack's *Poesie und Kunst der Araber in Spanien und Sicilien* (Berlin, 1865; second edition, Stuttgart, 1877) is largely out of date, but remains useful for its extensive verse translations.

Most active of contemporary students of Andalusian poetry is Emilio García Gómez, editor and translator of a number of important texts, author of perceptive studies of which the following are available in book form: *Poesía arábigoandaluza* (Madrid, 1952), *Cinco poetas musulmanes* (Madrid, 1944). He also surveys the entire development of Andalusian poetry in his introduction to *Poemas arábigoandaluces* (Madrid, 1930, 1943).

In *La Poésie andalouse en arabe classique au XIe siècle* (Paris, 1937, 1953), Henri Pérès is inclined to overstress non-Arab and non-Islamic elements, and his painstaking tabulation of poetic motifs may need to be corrected at some points for the effects of convention on one hand, of the peculiarities of some poets on the other; he does nevertheless sift and present in a masterly form an enormous amount of material pertaining to a key period.

The bulk of A. R. Nykl's *Hispano-Arabic Poetry and its Relations with the old Provençal Troubadours* (Baltimore, 1946) is a survey of Andalusian poetry period by period, with biographical notices of a great many poets and translations of selected passages. Surprisingly —for he gives ample evidence of extensive erudition—Nykl's translations from the Arabic are often very wide of the mark. His selections, too, appear to be influenced by strong personal likes and dislikes, and by his overriding interest in a link with Troubadour poetry—see also his *Troubadour Studies* (Cambridge, Mass., 1944). Yet there is a wealth of information in this work, not least in the bibliographical notes.

A pioneer work on strophic poetry is Martin Hartmann's *Das Arabische Strophengedicht. I: Das Muwaššah* (Weimar, 1897).

S. M. Stern's *Les Chansons mozarabes* (Palermo, 1953)—an attempt to decipher all the known *kharjas* composed in a mixture of Romance and Arabic—is one of several important contributions this author has made to the study of the *muwashshaḥ*, and he has announced his intention of publishing a comprehensive work on the subject.

Modern Arab scholars are showing a growing interest in al-Andalus. Among their books specifically dealing with literature may be noted: *az-Zajal fī 'l-Andalus*, a series of lectures by ʿAbd-al-ʿAzīz al-Ahwānī (Cairo, 1957); *Udabāʾ al-ʿArab fī 'l-Andalus wa-ʿAṣr al-Inbiʿāth* by Buṭrus al-Bustānī (Beirut, 1947); *Al-Adab al-Andalusī min al-Fatʾḥ ilā Suqūṭ al-Khilāfa* by Aḥmad Haykal (Cairo, 1958); *Tārīkh al-Adab al-Andalusī—ʿAṣr Siyādat Qurṭuba* by Iḥsān ʿAbbās (Beirut, 1960); *Fī 'l-Adab al-Andalusī* (Damascus, 1957) and *Aṭ-Ṭabīʿa fī 'sh-Shiʿr al-Andalusī* (Damascus, 1959) by Jawdat ar-Rikābī. Vol. 3 of Aḥmad Amīn's *Ẓuhr al-Islām* (Cairo, 1955) is devoted to al-Andalus.

Of Andalusian literary works in translation, one of the most useful is an anthology entitled *The Pennants* (*Rāyāt al-Mubarrizīn*) compiled by Ibn-Saʿīd in 1243. Although unequal in quality, and although only about half of the poems in it are by Andalusians, it is representative of the taste of the time. It forms the basis of García Gómez's *Poemas arábigoandaluces* (Madrid, 1930, 1943), and has been very ably translated into English verse by A. J. Arberry under the title *Moorish Poetry* (Cambridge, 1953). Several translations also exist of Ibn-Ḥazm's treatise on love, *The Ring of the Dove*, including two in English: one by Nykl in 1931, and a superior one by Arberry (London, 1953). Some fifty poems and one epistle by Ibn-Zaydūn are translated by Auguste Cour in *Un Poète arabe d'Andalousie* (Constantine, 1920), and the poems of Ibn az-Zaqqāq have been edited and translated by García Gómez (Madrid, 1956).

Abū Bakr at-Ṭurṭūshī's *Sirāj al-Mulūk* has been translated by Maximiliano Alarcón under the title of *Lámpara de los príncipes* (two volumes, Madrid, 1930); so has the *Risāla* of ash-Shaqundī: by García Gómez under the title of *Elogio del Islam español* (Granada, 1934), and by A. Luya in *Hesperis*, xxii (1936).

Ibn-Ṭufayl's *Ḥayy ibn-Yaqẓān* was first translated into English by S. Ockley as *The Improvement of Human Reason* (London, 1708), and this was revised by A. S. Fulton (London, 1929). A popular, abridged version entitled *The Awakening of the Soul*, by Paul Brönnle, was first published in 1904. It has also been translated into Spanish, as *El filósofo autodidacto*, by González Palencia (Madrid, 1934) and into French by Léon Gauthier (Beirut, 1936).

A popular traditional narrative has been edited and translated by García Gómez under the title *Un texto árabe occidental de la Leyenda de Alejandro* (Madrid, 1929).

INDEX

The Arabic article al-, with its variants such as an-, ash-, etc., is neglected in the alphabetical arrangement
Page numbers in italic indicate a reference to an illustration